FACE

Investigations of a Dog

Works from Five European Art Foundations

jrp|ringier

Table of contents

FACE: Five European Art Foundations

FACE (Foundation of Arts for a Contemporary Europe) is a European interest group for the arts formed in 2008 and established by five private non-profit art foundations in five different countries. This alliance is a unique collaboration dedicated to the promotion of contemporary art. The Partner Foundations believe that together they can achieve a wider platform from which to broaden and empower the scope of their activities through ambitious international art projects.

First presented at the European Parliament in Brussels in 2008, the FACE project is a not-for-profit exercise, born out of the need for private institutions to join forces and build on their resources for the support and development of contemporary art.

FACE aims to promote internationally emerging and more established artists from all over the world. In particular the group wants to focus on supporting the production and exhibition of new works. FACE Partner Foundations will support artists by helping them produce and exhibit their work, as well as focusing on bringing an ever-growing public closer to contemporary art and culture.

As a first initiative the group has jointly organized *Investigations of a Dog*, an exhibition that draws its title from a short story by Franz Kafka (1922) and presents artworks from the Partner Foundations' collections. During the course of two years, the exhibition travels to be hosted by the five foundations.

The future of FACE is one of a developing body that can reach out to other art institutions, both public and private, to facilitate and promote contemporary culture.

The FACE founding partners are: DESTE Foundation, Athens (Greece), Ellipse Foundation, Cascais (Portugal), Fondazione Sandretto Re Rebaudengo, Turin (Italy), La maison rouge – Fondation Antoine de Galbert, Paris (France), and Magasin 3 Stockholm Konsthall (Sweden).

Presentation of the Five Foundations

DESTE Foundation

Ellipse Foundation

Fondazione Sandretto Re Rebaudengo

La maison rouge – Fondation Antoine de Galbert

Magasin 3 Stockholm Konsthall

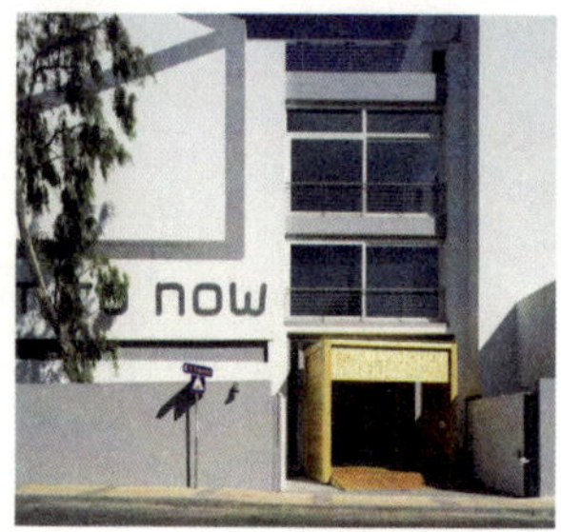

The DESTE Foundation
For Contemporary Art

Filellinon 11 & Em. Pappa street
Nea Ionia 142 34
Athens – Greece
www.deste.gr

The DESTE Foundation for Contemporary Art is a non-profit institution based in Athens, Greece. The Foundation was established in Geneva in 1983 by collector Dakis Joannou, together with curators Adelina von Fürstenberg and Efi Strousa. Ever since, DESTE has been organizing exhibitions and has been supporting projects and publications internationally.

Through an exhibition program that promotes emerging as well as established artists, the DESTE Foundation aims to broaden the audience for contemporary art, to enhance opportunities for young artists, and to explore the connections between contemporary art and culture. The flexibility of DESTE's exhibition schedule enables the Foundation to respond to what is current in the art world and to embark on interesting projects at short notice. DESTE's program also extends to curatorial projects and special events that explore the connections between art and fashion, music, film, architecture, design, and contemporary culture.

From its inception until 1998, DESTE organized and supported shows in Greece, Cyprus, and Switzerland. These shows include *Cultural Geometry* (1988), *Psychological Abstraction* (1989), *Artificial Nature* (1990), *Post Human* (1992–

1993), and *Everything That's Interesting Is New* (1996), a series of exhibitions that drew on the holdings of the Dakis Joannou Collection. In 1998, the DESTE Foundation moved to its first permanent space in Neo Psychico, Athens, where an ambitious exhibition program developed, including, among others, the shows *Global Vision* (1999), Jeff Koons' *A Millennium Celebration* (1999–2000), and Tim Noble and Sue Webster's *Masters of the Universe* (2000). As part of the Athens 2004 Cultural Program, the Deste Foundation mounted *Monument to Now*, the Foundation's most ambitious project to date, a group show with more than 60 participating artists, curated by Dan Cameron, Jeffrey Deitch, Alison Gingeras, Massimiliano Gioni, and Nancy Spector.

Since January 2006, DESTE has been housed in a renovated former sock factory in Nea Ionia, Athens. The exhibition program of the new space was inaugurated by *Panic Room* (2006–2007), a group show with works on paper from The Dakis Joannou Collection, and by the Yellow Room Projects *Anathena* (2006–2007) and *Part Time Punks* (2007), both of which were selected through an open submission. Recent DESTE shows include *Fractured Figure* (2007–2008), *A GUEST + A HOST = A GHOST* (2009), and *ALPHA OMEGA* (2010).

Apart from the shows that draw on works from the Dakis Joannou Collection, the DESTE Foundation also initiates a number of ongoing projects: the DESTE Prize, awarded biannually to an emerging Greek artist, the Hydra Slaughterhouse Project, and the destefashioncollection.

To further support its mission, DESTE has also established the Contemporary Greek Artists' Archive, a helpful resource for curators and researchers, as well as a specialized art library that is open to the public.

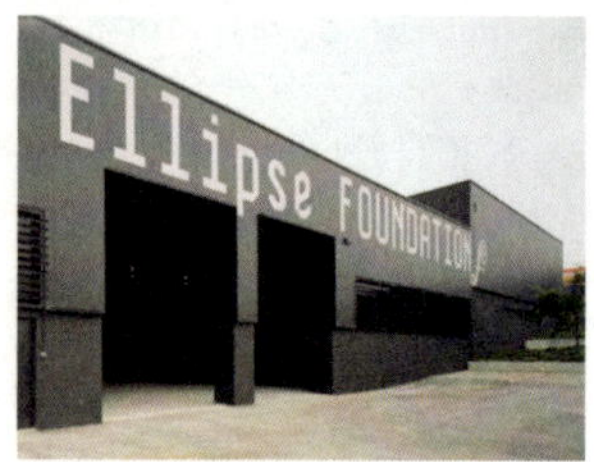

Ellipse Foundation |
Contemporary Art Collection

Alameda das Fisgas 79
Alcoitão 2645-117 Alcabideche
Cascais, Portugal
www.ellipsefoundation.com

The Ellipse Foundation was officially established in 2004 with the purpose of supporting contemporary artists through various initiatives, including acquisitions, the production of works of art, exhibitions, special projects, and educational programs.

The collection consists of around 900 works in various media—painting, drawing, sculpture, photography, film and video, and installation—and is representative of the key trends in international contemporary art over the last three decades. The collection has been organized around three main categories: seminal artists active since the 1970s, artists mid-way through their respective careers, and young and emerging artists in the 21st century.

Ellipse Foundation is the fruit of the initiative of João Oliveira Rendeiro, who began collecting privately during the 1980s. His dedication later evolved toward realizing the idea of creating a large and prestigious international collection of contemporary art in Portugal. The collection was built up through the work of a group of curators composed of Manuel González (JPMorgan Chase Art Collection, New York), Pedro Lapa (Museu do Chiado, Lisbon), and Alexandre Melo. The curators were assisted by a number of consultants, including, among others, Lars Grambye (Kunsthallen Brandts, Copenhagen), James Lingwood (Artangel, London)

Bartomeu Marí (MACBA, Barcelona), Hervé Mikaeloff (Paris), and Andrew Renton (Goldsmiths' College, London).

In 2006, the Ellipse Foundation inaugurated its Art Centre, a 3,500-square-meter converted warehouse in Alcabideche, with the exhibition *Open House* curated by Alexandre Melo, Pedro Lapa, and Manuel Gonzalez.

One of the major lines of the Ellipse Foundation has been collaboration with international curators, who have brought their own view on the collection. *Come, Come, Come Into My World* (2007–08), by Andrew Renton, focused on the physicality of the artwork and in the dialogues established between the object and the public. In Listen *Darling ... The World is Yours* (2008–09), Lisa Philips proposed a new look at gender issues and sexual identity, which characterize the social and cultural dynamics of our times.

In parallel, the foundation has developed several solo exhibitions and Project Rooms. In *Alice* (2007), Robert Wilson assumed as the starting point the famous tale of Lewis Carroll, to explore questions of space and light. Hedi Slimane's *Costa da Caparica 1989* (2007) retraced the intersections between art, culture, and youth in a re-definition of the ideal of masculinity. *Le Passeur* (2008), by Filipa César, examined the interception between fiction and reality in order to reflect on the construction of memory and identity. The Ellipse Foundation has also organized several exhibitions outside the Art Centre, for example *Edit!* (2007) in Coimbra, or *Young at Heart* (2008) in Cascais.

The main line that comes out from these exhibitions lies in the ability of the artists represented in the collection to generate reflections about some of the most important issues of our times.

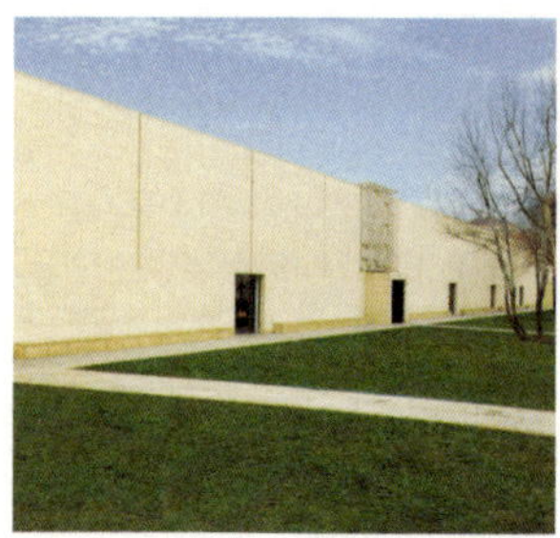

Fondazione Sandretto Re Rebaudengo

Via Modane, 16
10141 Turin – Italy
www.fsrr.org

The Italian contemporary art foundation Fondazione Sandretto Re Rebaudengo was founded in 1995 by the international contemporary art collector Patrizia Sandretto Re Rebaudengo and is under the artistic directorship of Francesco Bonami. The Fondazione's first exhibition space was set up in 1997 at the Palazzo Re Rebaudengo in Guarene d'Alba, a small town just outside Turin.

From as early as 1995, the Fondazione Sandretto Re Rebaudengo has been producing and showing the work of artists who have since gone on to become internationally acclaimed, such as Doug Aitken, Maurizio Cattelan, Damien Hirst, and Shirin Neshat. In September 2002, the Fondazione opened its current headquarters, a 3,500-square-meter center for contemporary art in Turin. The center is a flexible structure that presents challenging exhibitions, often of an experimental and site-responsive nature, covering political, social, and philosophical themes and issues, bringing together local, national, and international artists.

Exhibitions include *Don't touch the White Woman* in 2004; *T1 and T2*—1st and 2nd editions of the *Turin Triennial*, featuring the Takashi Murakami retrospective in 2005 and Paul Chan in 2008/9; *Sub-Contingent—The Indian Subcontinent in Contemporary Art* and *ALLLOOKSAME, Contemporary Art from China, Japan and Korea* in 2006; and *Greenwashing: Environment. Perils, Promises and Perplexities* in 2008, as well as co-projects with other international art institutions such as the Hara Museum in Tokyo (*Chain of Visions*, 2001), the Serpentine Gallery in London (Doug Aitken, *New Ocean*, 2003), the Walker Art Center in Minneapolis (*How Latitudes Become Forms*, 2003), the Baltic Mill in Gateshead (*Carol Rama*, 2004), and Tate Liverpool (*Glenn Brown*, 2009).

Fondazione Sandretto Re Rebaudengo also offers a wide-ranging program of activities and events (films, talks, music, theater, performance, and dance) that are organized in parallel and in response to all the main shows.

The Fondazione has an educational department to accommodate local schools and runs courses for adults about contemporary art, as well as providing a team of art mediators situated within the exhibition space, who are always on hand to further explain the concept of each exhibition and talk about individual works with visitors. The Fondazione also organizes an annual Young Curators Residency Program as well as an annual international Prize (Premio StellaRe) honouring women's achievements across the world.

The Sandretto Re Rebaudengo Collection was started in the early 1990s and is still constantly evolving today. It consists of over 1,000 contemporary works of art in various media by both internationally acclaimed and emerging artists.

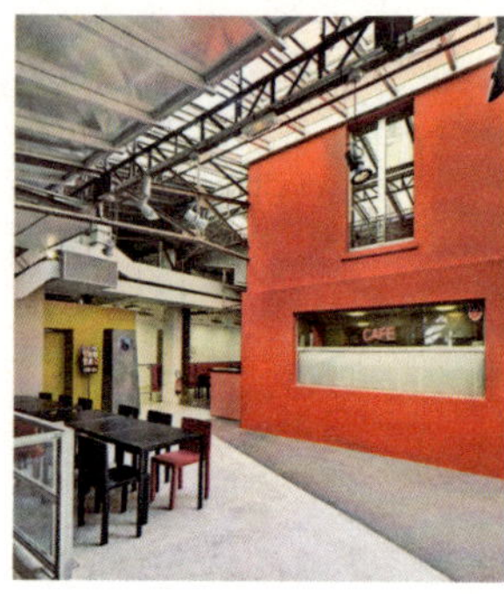

La maison rouge –
Fondation Antoine de
Galbert

10, boulevard de la Bastille
75012 Paris – France
www.lamaisonrouge.org

La maison rouge, a private non-profit foundation, opened in June 2004 in Paris. Its purpose is to promote the different facets of contemporary creation through a program of temporary exhibitions, some of which are staged by independent curators. Functioning as an art center, its vocation is to explore the diversity of contemporary artistic experimentation and expression by way of solo and thematic shows and special exhibitions focusing on selected private collections. Through each art experience that it incites and initiates, the foundation aims to encourage multiple attitudes, practices, and approaches to contemporary creation, opening the doors to such different forms of expression as outsider art, performance, primitive art, or popular art. This diversity reflects the personality and taste of La maison rouge's founder, Antoine de Galbert, an art collector and active figure on the French art scene.

Beginning with *L'Intime (Behind Closed Doors: The Private Life of Collections)* in 2004, La maison rouge regularly stages exhibitions on the theme of private collections and the issues and questions surrounding them. Particular focus is placed on individuals with a strong, personal vision, allowing surprises and discoveries. Past displays include the outsider art collection of Arnulf Rainer, video art from Isabelle and Jean-Conrad Lemaitre's collection, and Latin American art from Isabel and Agustín Coppel's collection.

Over the past few years, La maison rouge has also presented solo shows by Ann Hamilton, Christian Boltanski, Henry Darger, Gregor Schneider, Berlinde de Bruyckere, and Mika Rottenberg, as well as thematic exhibitions such as *Sots Art: Political Art in Russia since the 70s*; *Vraoum! Comics and Contemporary Art*; *Vinyl, Records and Covers by Artists*.

Publications include monographs, exhibition catalogues, and art history reference books, certain of which are edited by La maison rouge's active and dynamic Society of Friends.

The foundation extends over 2,000 square meters on the site of a disused factory built around a former house "la maison rouge" or "red house," from which the venue takes its name. A special program in an open-air courtyard at the heart of the foundation offers an occasion for invited artists to create commissioned work.

La maison rouge seeks to extend the circle of initiates and enrich visitors' experience through guided visits, lectures, and special events such as concerts or performances. Interaction and exchanges with artists, art historians, collectors, curators, and thinkers from all fields create opportunities to explore the exhibited works from a given perspective. These situate the works in the history of art and ideas, but also in relation to the art world today.

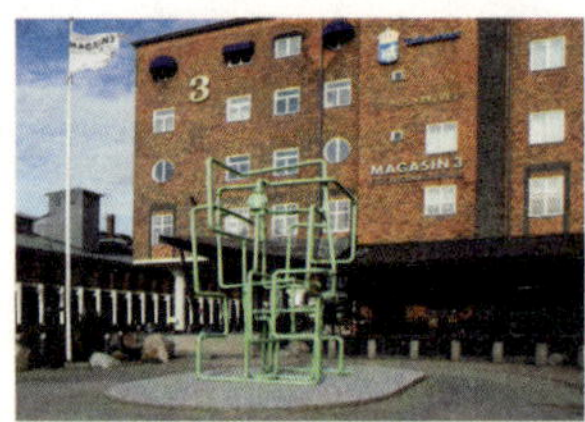

Magasin 3 Stockholm
Konsthall

Frihamnen, SE-115 56
Stockholm – Sweden
www.magasin3.com

Magasin 3 Stockholm Konsthall was established in 1987 and has, since its inception, been recognized for major exhibitions presenting works by internationally established artists, as well as for mid-career presentations. The aim is to actively participate in contemporary culture by introducing and presenting artists and supporting artistic work. The exhibition program of Magasin 3 is regarded as a complement and challenge to other institutions of contemporary art in Europe. Over the last 20 years the institution has presented legendary solo exhibitions by such artists as Felix Gonzalez-Torres, Agnes Martin, Bruce Nauman, Chris Burden, Katharina Grosse, Mona Hatoum, Pipilotti Rist, Annika von Hausswolff, Christian Boltanski, and Santiago Sierra.

Magasin 3 produces and presents approximately six exhibitions every year. This often involves the commissioning and production of new works. The first exhibitions also marked the beginning of the collection. A close dialectical relationship between exhibition program and collection has become significant for the institution. The collection of Magasin 3 Stockholm Konsthall currently consists of approximately 600 works of art. The focus is on three-dimensional, site-specific, and photography and video based works. Acquisitions are made in conjunction with the exhibitions as well as outside the exhibition program.

Through close collaboration with artists and institutions, the collection is in constant progress. Works from the collection are presented at Magasin 3 in solo exhibitions by the artists represented, as well as in thematic shows; they are also shown in numerous museums around the world as the result of an active lending program. James Turrell's *Dawning* (1992), is the only work that is permanently installed.

In conjunction with the exhibitions, Magasin 3 publishes catalogues documenting the exhibited works and the artists' production. In the last few years Magasin 3 has expanded its program to include lectures and talks that complement the publications in providing a more in-depth view of the exhibitions.

Magasin 3 Stockholm Konsthall is one of Europe's leading institutions for contemporary art. It is located in a former warehouse from the 1920s in the old Freeport district of Stockholm, with an exhibition space of 1500 square meters. Robert Weil, a leading Swedish industrialist, is the founding chairman of the board. David Neuman has been the director since its inception. Magasin 3 is an independent cultural institution under the auspices of the privately owned company group Proventus AB (www.proventus.se).

An Introduction to the Exhibition

Irene Calderoni, curator
Fondazione Sandretto Re Rebaudengo, Turin

The exhibition *Investigations of a Dog* draws its title from a 1922 short story by Franz Kafka. Still a puppy, a dog suffers an identity crisis that brings him to question his own nature and, more generally, the canine essence. Endowed with a more solitary, introverted temperament than other dogs who happily live together without asking themselves questions, the protagonist embarks on a quest for knowledge that takes him to the margins of society, and turns him into a madman, or a stranger in the eyes of others. Paradoxically, this isolation is in fact the expression of an extreme form of love of the investigator dog toward his fellows, because it is out of his concern for others that he is trying to understand what it means to be a dog.

This short story, and more generally the themes and expressive strategies that recur in Franz Kafka's works, have inspired the selection of the works in the exhibition. They all center around the question of how linguistic innovation can entail a political dimension to art making that precedes the content-related aspects of the artwork. The French philosophers Deleuze and Guattari, in their analysis of Kafka's work, have come up with the notion of "minor" literature to describe this link between writing and politics, i.e. the possibility for artistic creation to carry revolutionary messages, starting precisely with the subversive use of language. Minor here means that something is not official, not in power, but nonetheless moves within the domain of power to find escape lines, to create spaces of freedom. Minor is the use of a major language by a minority—take Kafka, a Jew from Prague writing in German: language is de-territorialized, ceases to be the expression of a national identity, and becomes nomadic. Minor means establishing a link between individual events and a larger context, finding the political relevance of individual stories. Finally, minor is the collective nature of an utterance, the transition from individual to collective voice. The artists brought together here share a practice of art that can be read in the light of this category of minor. They have initiated an "eccentric" art discourse, which cannot be associated with any of the acquired aesthetic categories, and subverts the conventional use of the expressive means it adopts. This formal research, however, is not an end in itself, but looks at the outside world, connects with the political situation of its time—i.e. is socially active. From this perspective, appropriating objects and signs from extra-artistic fields, and attributing new meanings and functions to them, is a key strategy, employed by many of the artists in the exhibition to reflect upon central themes in contemporary society, such as postcolonial identity, gender, race and religious conflicts, violence and collective paranoia, economic disparities and the excesses of consumer society, the sense of community and the condition of marginality, the relationship between memory and present time. The gesture of appropriating and de-locating interrupts the codified relationship of signification, enabling an analysis of stereotypes and acquired traditions. The hybridization of aesthetic visions peculiar to contexts that are far apart from each other—low- and highbrow, official and alternative culture—creates an effect of estrangement that subverts the usual ways of looking at reality. The registers of the incongruous, paradoxical, grotesque, ironic, and uncanny are all devices used by the artists to investigate the world around them, and hand it back to us for a critical evaluation. The use of obsolete media, of outdated techniques and expressive forms, serves the function of recovering memories lost in social history. The exploration of the boundaries between fiction and reality, the artificial staging of reality and, conversely, the pseudo-scientific documentation of fictitious situations, is a way of questioning the acquired notions of truth and falseness. The process-oriented, performative nature of the works in which artists limit their intervention to the activation of a mechanism the effects of which escape their control, refuses individual forms of utterance.

These and other strategies enacted by the artists in the exhibition produce expressive forms that are directly focused on content and allow for a possible revolutionary use of the language of art. Like the canine protagonist in Kafka's short story, these artists ask themselves questions about the meaning of art making, spurred on by a passionate emotional involvement in human society.

List of Artists

Vasco Araújo, Virginie Barré, Philippe Bazin,
Mircea Cantor, Maurizio Cattelan, Roberto
Cuoghi, Mark Dion, Gardar Eide Einarsson,
Urs Fischer, Fischli & Weiss, Claire Fontaine,
David Hammons, Annika von Hausswolff,
Thomas Hirschhorn, William Kentridge, Kimsooja,
Jeff Koons, Sigalit Landau, Sherrie Levine,
DeAnna Maganias, Mark Manders, Esko Männikkö,
Marepe, Paul McCarthy, Boris Mikhailov,
Bruce Nauman, Cady Noland, Martin Parr, Navin
Rawanchaikul, Aurel Schmidt, Gregor Schneider,
Lara Schnitger, Santiago Sierra, Lorna Simpson,
Stéphane Thidet, Kara Walker.

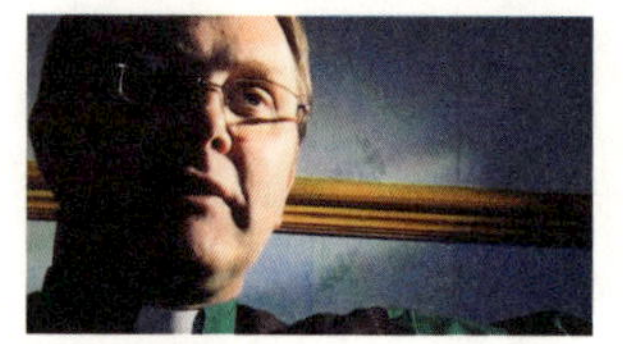

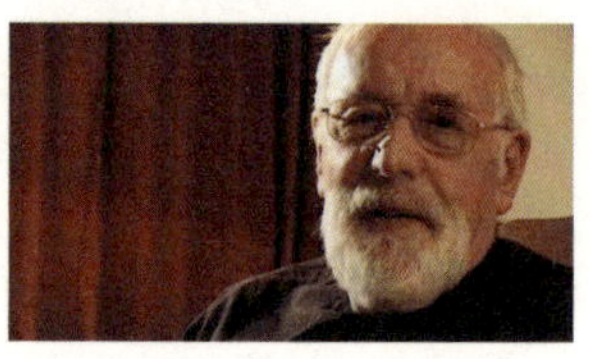

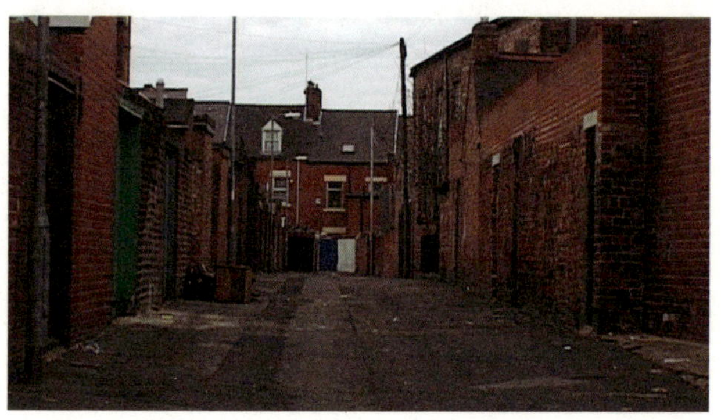

VASCO ARAÚJO

Born in 1975 in Lisbon (Portugal), he lives and works in Lisbon.

Vasco Araújo explores issues such as cultural and sexual identity, analyzing in particular the stereotypes created by society. For his narrative references or topics, Araújo often draws inspiration from opera, in which he finds a world of masks, costumes, and divas, an artificial, made-up universe, always excessive when it comes to the reconstruction of clichés. The video *About Being Different* is the result of the artist's residence in Newcastle Gateshead, and of his collaboration with the parishioners of the local community. It examines the ideas of community and marginality, and is inspired by Benjamin Britten's opera *Peter Grimes* (1945), which deals with a fisherman persecuted by his village. After showing Britten's opera to five local parishioners, Araújo interviewed them and recorded their comments on what it means to be different inside a small community such as that of Gateshead.

About Being Different, 2007
Video; color, sound; 18'24"
Ellipse Foundation – Contemporary Art Collection, Cascais

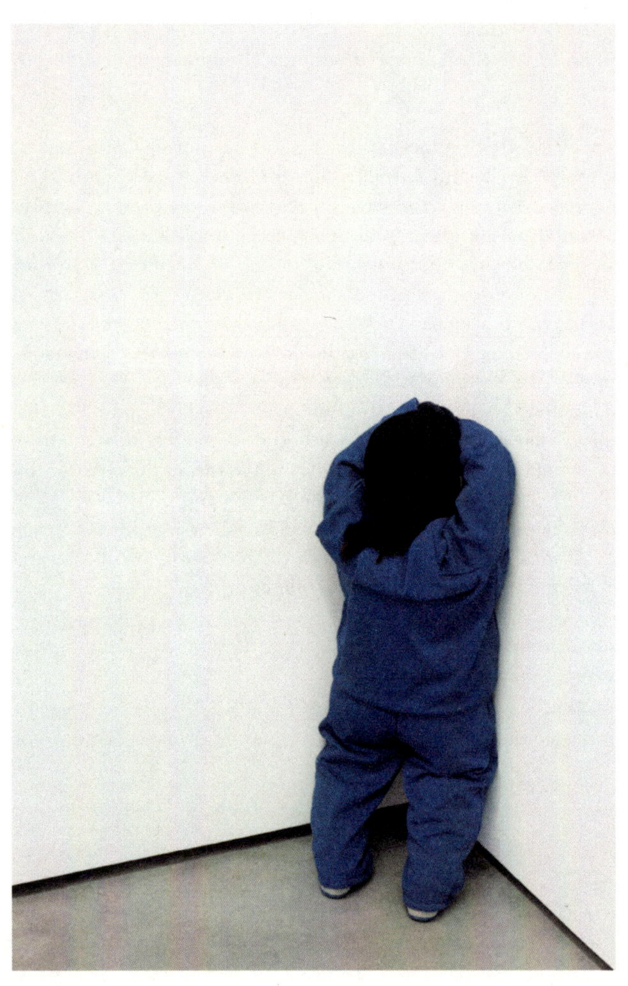

VIRGINIE BARRÉ
Born in 1970 in Quimper (France), she lives and works in Douarnenez (France).

Virginie Barré appropriates the aesthetics of everyday life and mass culture, famous characters and popular stories from comics, movies, and news alike, deforming them and making them ambiguous through drawings, sculptures, and installations that explore the themes of death and collective paranoia. The artist models unsettling images suspended between what is known and what is impossible to identify. Barré's worlds are often peopled by mannequins and dolls, the epitome of that mysterious territory where reality and fiction blend. *Les Hommes venus d'ailleurs* eludes our gaze, as well as any relationship with the spectator. The figures' proportions and clothing enhance this effect of estrangement, reinforcing the purpose of not letting yourself be caged into any pre-determined categories, even if it means becoming totally isolated.

Sans titre, « Les Hommes venus d'ailleurs », 2005
Sculpture; cloth, foam; 110 x 40 x 40 cm
Collection Antoine de Galbert, La maison rouge, Paris

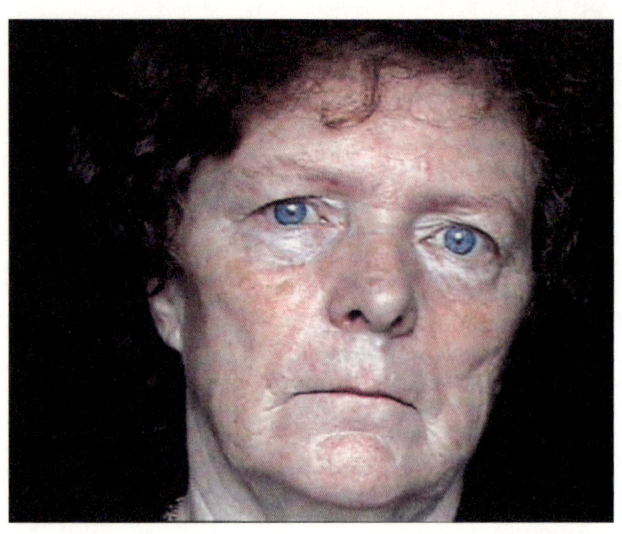

PHILIPPE BAZIN
Born in 1954 in Nantes (France), he lives and works in
Paris.

The career of artist Philippe Bazin began when, while working as a physician, he started to photograph his patients,
and created a series of disturbing portraits in which elderly
and sick people, who are usually relegated to the margins
of society, look back at the observer, challenging them.
Une heure de travail is part of a video series the artist
created during his artist-in-residence stay at the Scottish
distillery William Grant & Sons in 2002. The company, nes-
tled in the heart of a valley, has business relations all over
the world. Developing his research into the relationship
between individual lives and the institutional system,
Philippe Bazin videoed eight employees of the firm, in a single, static, hour-long shot in close-up. Each employee
stared at the camera without moving or speaking for the
entire duration. The result is a poignant work in-between
photography and documentary, which explores a new
approach to the portrait: how much can you learn of this
person's life by staring at her for a long period of time.

Une heure de travail, «Dufftown, n°9, Ecosse», 2002
Video; color; 60'
Collection Antoine de Galbert, La maison rouge, Paris

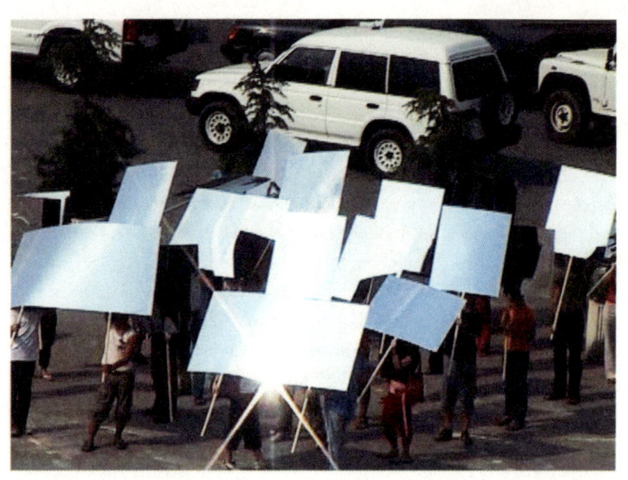

MIRCEA CANTOR

Born in 1977 in Oradea (Romania), he lives and works on Earth.

Mircea Cantor investigates the impact of individual acts of rebellion by people who are forced to operate every day within complex political and bureaucratic structures. Both in his videos and in his sculptures, Cantor opts for essential formal choices, which nevertheless reveal a strong communicative impact. *The Landscape Is Changing* is a video documentation of a performance, in which a group of people stages a silent protest march through the streets of the Albanian capital Tirana. In Albania, until recently a communist state, demonstrations are rare and still strongly associated with propaganda parades for former dictator Enver Hoxha. Replacing the demonstrators' banners with mirrored surfaces, Cantor interrupts and short-circuits the demonstration's traditional information flow, sending back to bystanders fragments of the reality that surrounds them.

The Landscape Is Changing, 2003
Video; color, sound; 22'
Collection Magasin 3 Stockholm Konsthall

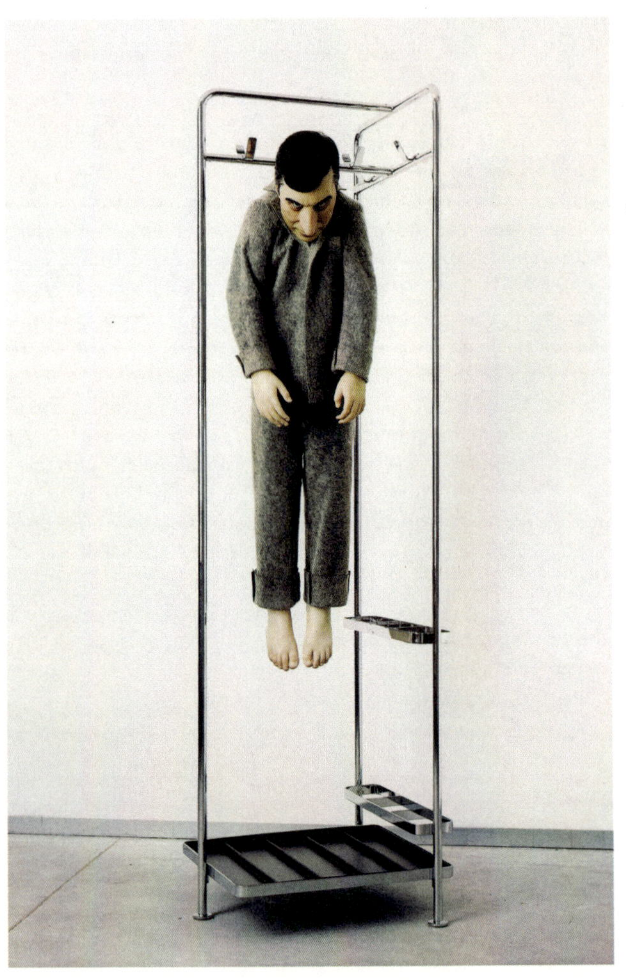

MAURIZIO CATTELAN
Born in 1960 in Padua (Italy), he lives and works in New York.

Maurizio Cattelan's works always cause controversy. He has been described as a master of provocation as well as a buffoon for his irreverent examination of the art world, often portrayed as a prison from which the artist is trying to escape. In *La Rivoluzione siamo noi*, a miniature version of the artist is hung from a coat rack designed by modernist architect Marcel Breuer. The suit Cattelan wears is made of felt, a material that refers to the work of German artist Joseph Beuys. In 1972, Beuys portrayed himself in the act of walking. This image, entitled *La Rivoluzione siamo noi*, expressed the energy and activism typical of Beuys' art. Cattelan, too, puts himself directly into his work, but with a very different attitude and purpose. While Beuys embodies the mythical figure of the artist as shaman, effecting a real change in society, Cattelan's attitude is playful and sarcastic as he underlines the impossibility of the action the artist is forced to carry out.

← *La Rivoluzione siamo noi*, 2000
Installation; mixed media; 190 x 47 x 52 cm
Collection Fondazione Sandretto Re Rebaudengo, Turin

Untitled (Natale 95) Stella con BR, 1995
Neon, 38 x 82 x 4 cm
Collection Fondazione Sandretto Re Rebaudengo, Turin

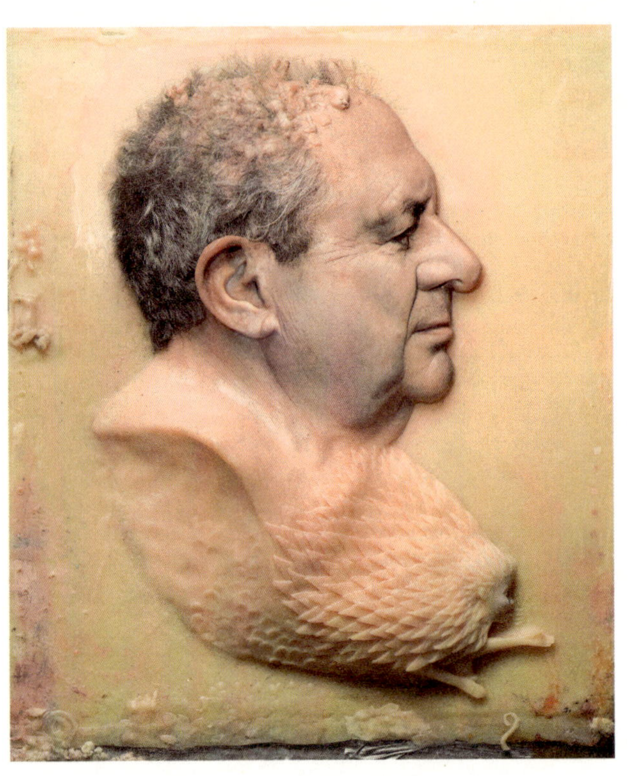

ROBERTO CUOGHI
Born in 1973 in Modena (Italy), he lives and works in Milan.

Metamorphosis, the idea of constant transformation and hybridization among forms and identities, is both a theme and an expressive strategy in the work of Roberto Cuoghi, who uses his own body, as well as classic media such as painting and drawing. *Untitled (Lady Godzilla)* is the result of a complicated production process, in which the final image is arrived at through the layering of multiple supports, which are then painted with different techniques and materials. This method yields an upsetting creature with a human face and an animal body that evokes the profile of the mythical Japanese dinosaur. Similarly, *MEGAS DAKIS* portrays the face of art collector Dakis Joannou, elaborating it into the terrifying forms of a harpy, the cruel bird-woman of Greek mythology. Cuoghi blends black humor (a constant hallmark of his work) with references to past and current cultures and political visions.

← *MEGAS DAKIS*, 2007
Print on cotton paper; 73 x 63.5 cm
The Dakis Joannou Collection

Untitled (Lady Godzilla), 2004
Gypsum, charcoal, enamel, acrylic; 50 x 35 cm
The Dakis Joannou Collection

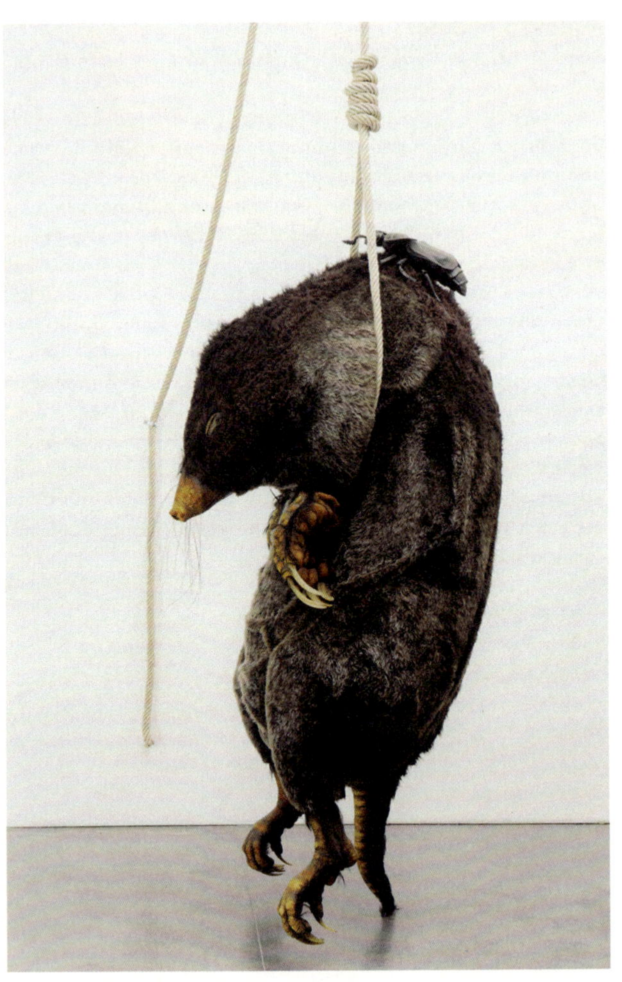

MARK DION

Born in 1961 in New Bedford (Massachusetts, USA), he lives and works in Pennsylvania.

Mark Dion turned a personal hobby of his—the natural sciences—into a privileged vantage point from which to examine the cultural representations of nature. The artist is especially fascinated by the historical figure of the amateur scientist, the dilettante of 18th and 19th centuries. In his sculpture *Les Nécrophores*, the unusual combination of a giant dead mole with a carrion beetle (necrophagous insects) on its back, was inspired by the experiments of Jean-Henri Fabre, a self-taught scientist from the 19th century, "half La Fontaine, half Cuvier," who spent his life studying entomology. Mark Dion transforms a scientific engraving documenting one of Fabre's experiments into a monumental installation that questions the distinction between scientific (rational) methods and subjective (irrational) influences. The mole, at the same time grotesque and scary, becomes a monster, closer to the atmosphere of children's stories than to scientific inquiry.

Les Nécrophores – L'Enterrement (Hommage à Jean-Henri Fabre), 1997
Resin cast, synthetic fur, rope; 250 x 125 x 140 cm
Collection Antoine de Galbert, La maison rouge, Paris

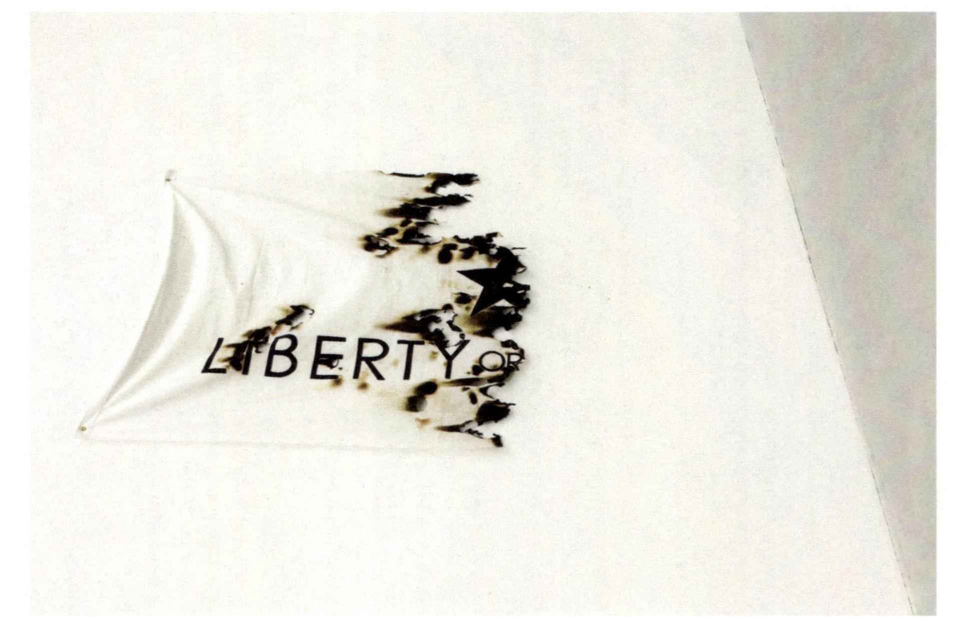
LIBERTY OR

GARDAR EIDE EINARSSON
Born in 1976 in Oslo (Norway), he lives and works in New York.

Gardar Eide Einarsson appropriates the signs that circulate through contemporary society in order to analyze their ideological content and functioning mechanisms. The artist mixes up the original cultural contexts, stealing images from mainstream culture—such as well-known corporate logos—as well as from subcultures—graffiti or punk music, for example. In his paintings, drawings, and installations, Einarsson triggers a short circuit between verbal language and the visual dimension, trying to show how the appearance of a text can complicate its codified message. *Burnt White Flag* digs a space between the institutional form of the flag and the emancipation conveyed by the text. A third element, the half-burnt fabric, alludes to a subversive action, an aggressive protest, which, however, remains ambiguous in terms of its intentions and results.

Burnt White Flag, 2005
Cotton and grommets; 165 x 149.8 cm
Ellipse Foundation – Contemporary Art Collection, Cascais

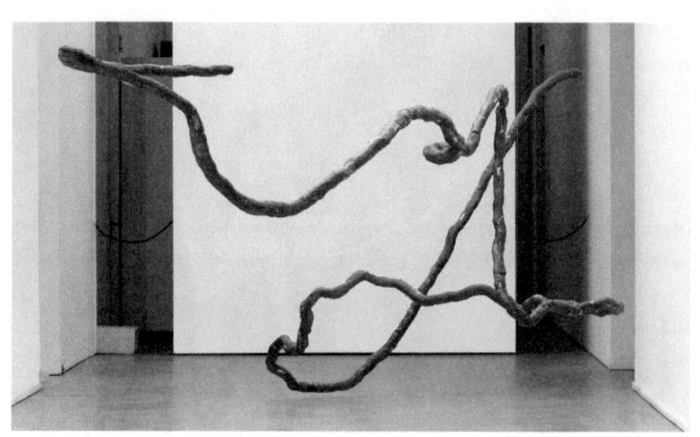

URS FISCHER
Born in 1973 in Zurich (Switzerland), he lives and works in
Zurich and New York.

Urs Fischer's works transform the ordinary into something
extraordinary. Trivial, everyday objects are deprived of
their functional purpose and endowed with unique aesthetic
and formal qualities. Fischer uses drawing, sculpture, and
installation to gradually alter nature—a process in which
the role of the artist is that of triggering the mechanism
and letting himself be surprised by the result, as if the
work had a life of its own. A disquieting vitality seems to
animate his linear sculptures, of which *Mackintosch Staccato* is an example. They reveal Fischer's obsession with
the line, an essential, abstract form, and a founding element of different artistic expressions. Fischer models this
simple form three-dimensionally, endowing it with energy
and an organic, visceral quality.

Mackintosh Staccato, 2006
Epoxy resin, pigment, enamel; 250 × 904 × 248 cm
The Dakis Joannou Collection

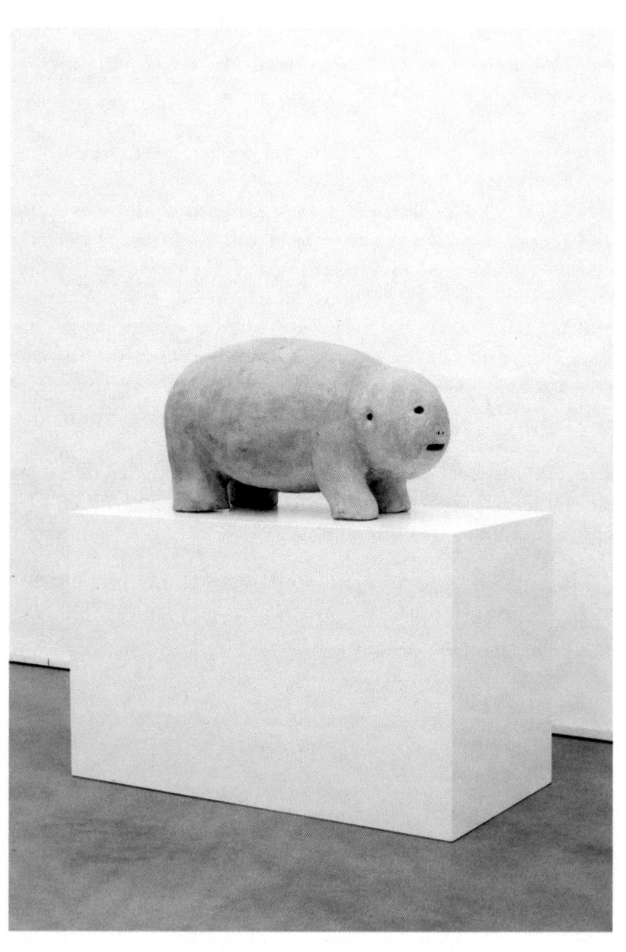

PETER FISCHLI & DAVID WEISS

Born in 1952 and 1946, both in Zurich (Switzerland), they have worked together since 1979. They live and work in Zurich.

The Swiss duo Fischli & Weiss have always chosen everyday life as their main subject, revealing unusual aspects of it, or distorting its meaning in such a way as to create intriguing, humorous situations. A playful, sometimes childish tone characterizes all the forms they work with, from sculpture to photography to video. In *Animal*, the artists operate in the space between the work's formal aspects and its title. The figure represented here does not exactly correspond to an animal, yet it does not completely differ from a vague idea of "animality," either. The work undermines the institutionalized relationship between signifier and signified, between the object and its definition, between the individual and its attribution to a community. In *Animal*, Fischli & Weiss use humor to touch on issues that are central to the anthropological/cultural debate, such as the notions of identity and otherness.

Animal, 1986
Polyurethane, cloth, paint; 55.8 x 96.5 x 98.4 cm
The Dakis Joannou Collection

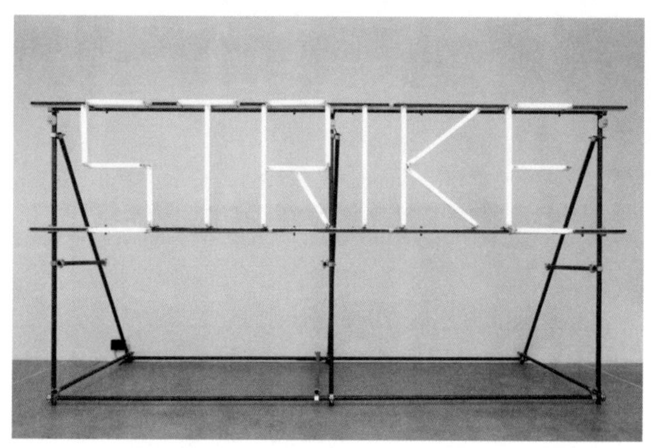
STRIKE

CLAIRE FONTAINE

Claire Fontaine is a Paris-based collective, founded in 2004.

Claire Fontaine is a collective artist—a self-described, single, readymade artist—whose name is the result of the appropriation of a famous French stationery brand. The artist duo often uses neon signs but, unlike the Conceptual and Minimalist traditions, these are infused with political and social content.

Indeed, this type of fluorescent light, traditionally found in public spaces such as schools, offices, and factories, evokes the labyrinthine spaces of institutional power around which Kafka's work revolves. Playing with the visitors' expectations and deception, the sculpture switches off as soon as it detects any motion around it, almost as if it wanted to "go on strike" in the presence of the public. Conversely, it signals the absence of movement by lighting up—stillness being the condition inherent in the definition of "strike" as a possible strategy to fight the museum as a place of institutional power.

Strike V. II, 2005–2007
Neon sculpture on scaffolding; 620 x 320 x 220 cm
Collection Antoine de Galbert, La maison rouge, Paris

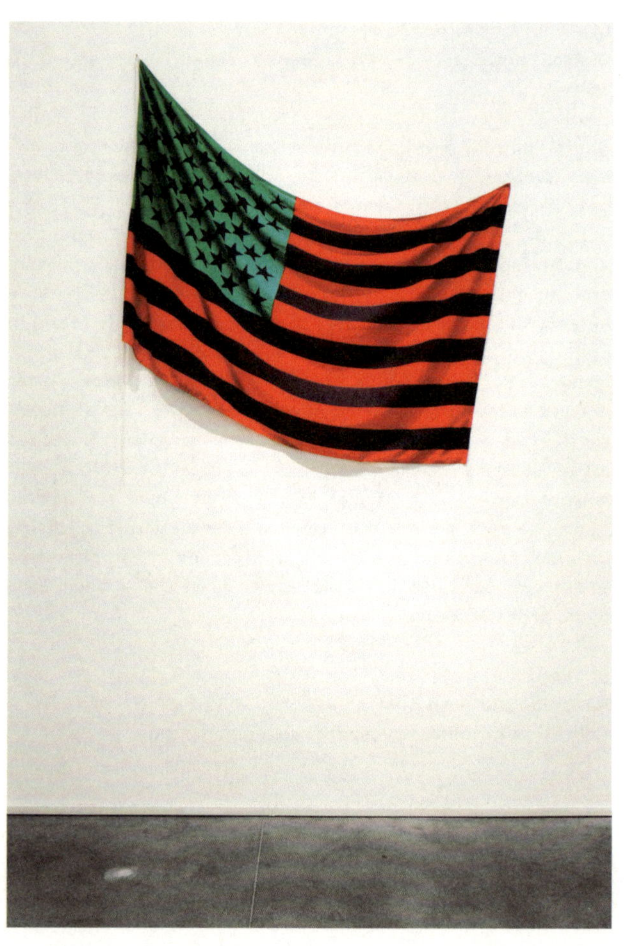

DAVID HAMMONS
Born in 1943 in Springfield (Illinois, USA), he lives and works
in New York.

Since the 1970s David Hammons has developed a minimal
aesthetics, which consists of works and interventions that
exploit limited resources to tackle complex issues, such as
those of race and the construction of difference in contemporary society. Hammons uses strategies such as disso-
nant associations and paradoxes to question commonplaces
and their effects on individuals.
In *African-American Flag*, the US flag takes on the hues of
Africa. This gesture, in its simplicity, creates a new object
thick with connotations, a symbol that does not exist, and
yet can be deciphered by looking at the history of the peo-
ples and nations it involves. The startling effect resulting
from the juxtaposition of contradictory elements is also
central in *Untitled*, a Japanese kimono installed in a display
cabinet as if it were a museum piece. The solemn garment,
however, conceals a filthy, bloodstained piece of under-
wear—an act of profanation that turns the exotic object
into a debased shred of reality.

← *African-American Flag*, 1990
Dyed cotton fabric; 142.2 x 223.5 cm
Ellipse Foundation – Contemporary Art Collection, Cascais

Untitled, 1995–2002
Japanese theater kimono, slip with bloodstains, and lollipop
in vitrine; 198 x 149 x 22.5 cm
Ellipse Foundation – Contemporary Art Collection, Cascais

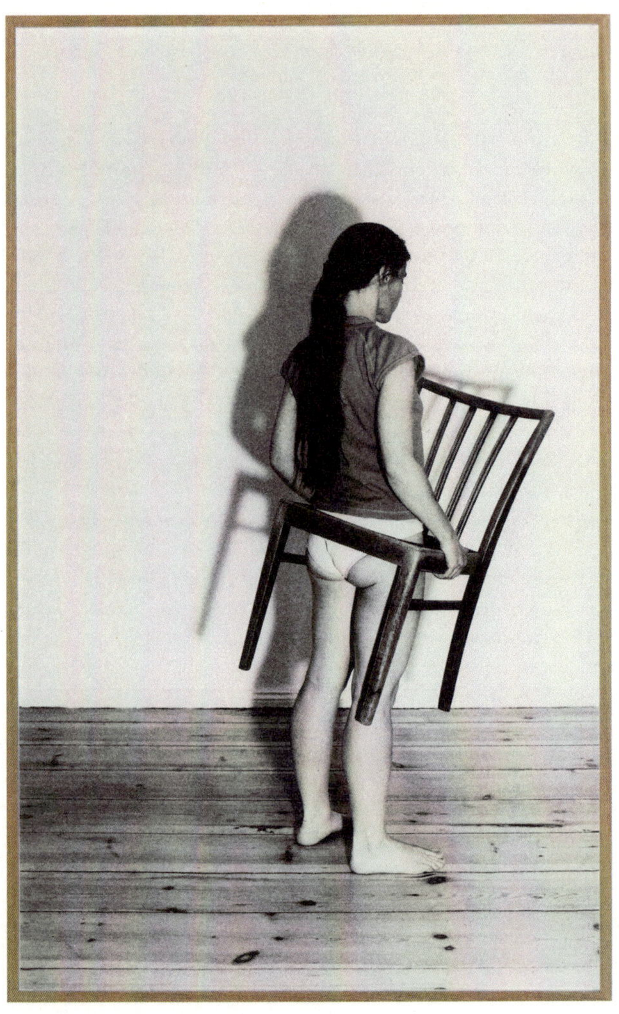

ANNIKA VON HAUSSWOLFF
Born in 1967 in Gothenburg (Sweden), she lives and works
in Gothenburg.

Annika von Hausswolff carefully composes photographs in
which the human body is often physically present or tangi-
ble only through the traces left behind. Contradictory feelings of unease and curiosity evoked by her macabre stories
and glimpses of the unexpected in the everyday have been
characteristics of von Hausswolff's work since the 1990s.
The female universe is often central to her investigation,
and is examined through the power structures that define
and constrain it in specific roles. In her work the female
body is often treated as an object, or abandoned in sinister landscapes evoking scenes of crime. Using well-known
motifs and art historical references, Annika von Hausswolff's work exists on the border between the documentary
and the staged.

Back to Nature, 1992
C-print mounted on paper; 43 x 60.5 cm
Collection Magasin 3 Stockholm Konsthall

← *Live From the Ocean*, 2005
Silver gelatin print; 166.5 x 101 cm
Collection Magasin 3 Stockholm Konsthall

Psyk:oanalys, 2009
Scanned collage on Lambdaprint; 55 x 42.5 cm
Collection Magasin 3 Stockholm Konsthall

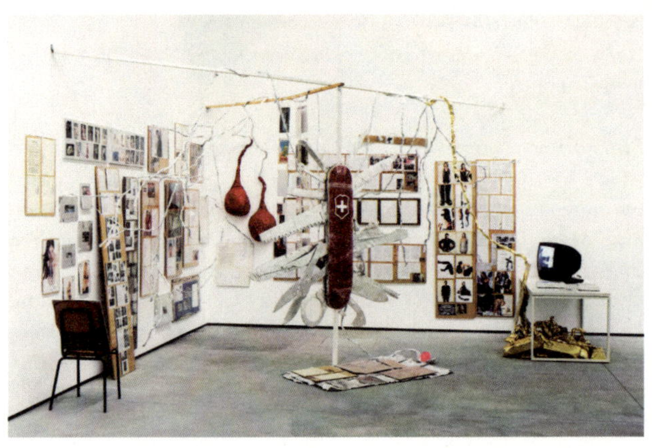

THOMAS HIRSCHHORN

Born in 1957 in Bern (Switzerland), he lives and works in Paris.

The sculptures and installations of Thomas Hirschhorn take as their subject the political and social reality of our time. The artist creates three-dimensional thought maps that contain information, accumulated layer upon layer until it turns into a sculptural presence and invades the space. The central element in *Spin Off* is a giant Swiss army knife, from which aluminum foil tentacles branch out and settle on drawings, photographs, collages, and other objects. Hirschhorn ironically encapsulates Swiss identity in the knife, while the use of recycled materials found in his living environment contradicts the stereotype of Switzerland as the homeland of luxury and well-being. Hirschhorn ridicules this myth with the help of a micro-galaxy of materials, objects, texts, current and historical themes—a complex web of references through which visitors are encouraged to find their way by making choices.

Spin Off, 1998
Mixed media installation; variable dimensions
Collection Fondazione Sandretto Re Rebaudengo, Turin

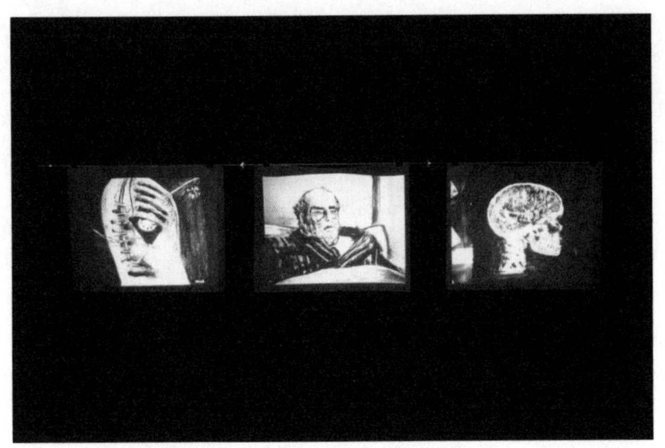

WILLIAM KENTRIDGE
Born in 1955 in Johannesburg (South Africa), he lives and works in Johannesburg.

Using an intense, poetic language, William Kentridge explores themes of violence, oppression, death, and rebirth in the history of South Africa. The technique he chooses for his works is the classic step-by-step animation method—only in this case the drawing is partly erased and redrawn with each frame, instead of being replaced by a new one, the final result being animations that "thrive upon" the remains of what came before. In *History of the Main Complaint*, Kentridge stages a backward journey, portraying a middle-aged entrepreneur named Soho (a recurring character in his works) as he lies on his deathbed. Slowly, the symbols of Soho's bureaucratic power start resurfacing in his mind, the very same symbols that have caused his agony. The video is a meditation on the contradictions of post-apartheid contemporary South Africa, still plagued by deep divisions that prevent a full recovery.

History of the Main Complaint, 1996
3-channel video installation; color, sound; 5'50 loop
Collection Fondazione Sandretto Re Rebaudengo, Turin

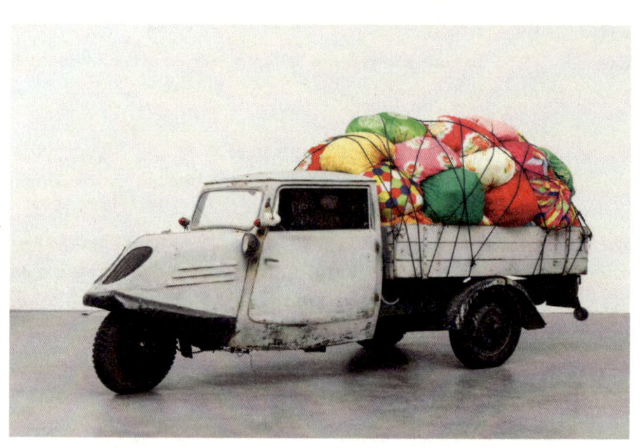

KIMSOOJA
Born in 1952 in Taegu (South Korea), she lives and works in
New York.

Kimsooja looks at individuals as they face an evolving
world, and imbues traditional forms with new meanings.
Bottari Truck is laden with bottaris, i.e. bundles made from
cloth, traditionally used to carry personal possessions,
especially on long trips or when moving, by force or free
will, in Korea. In 1997 Kimsooja traveled through her former home country on a similar truck. She rebuilds the
symbolic web in which these objects are entwined, exploring
the conditions of Korean women as well as of nomadism,
which frees cultural identity from a physical place. *Bottari
Truck* tells these stories not as a static sculptural work,
but as a process-oriented object that uses the performing
act of the artist to cross space and time, sewing together,
just like a needle, the edges of past and present memories,
individual and collective experiences.

Bottari Truck, 2005
Installation; truck, clothes, Korean bedcovers, elastic cord;
200 x 185 x 430 cm
Collection Magasin 3 Stockholm Konsthall

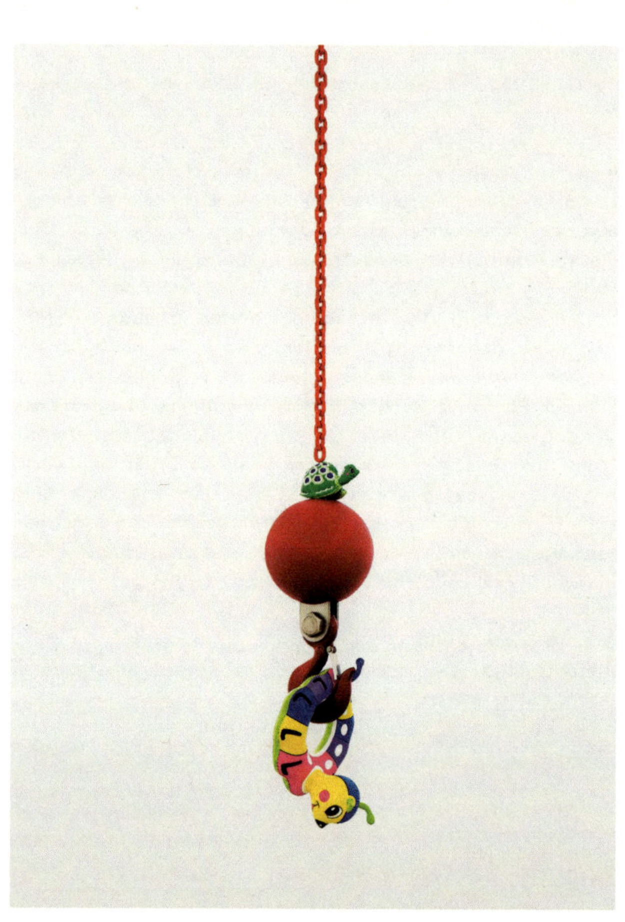

JEFF KOONS

Born in 1955 in York (Pennsylvania, USA), he lives and works in New York.

Since the 1980s Jeff Koons has been famous for works that display an ambiguous status between high art and the mass-produced goods of consumer society. The artist appropriates the symbols of American mass culture, be they pop stars or basketballs, estranging them from their context and celebrating their kitsch. *Wrecking Ball* is one of a series of sculptures in which ordinary objects, easy to find in any supermarket, such as colorful inflatable swimming-pool toys, are transformed in their material substance. Through an almost alchemical process, stainless steel copies of the toys are created and painted over so as to be indistinguishable from their originals. The artist views these works as Trojan horses, in that their appearance deceives the spectators' eye, and therefore betrays their expectations, triggering a paradoxical effect.

Wrecking Ball, 2002
Polychromed aluminum, carbon steel (coating), steel, and vinyl; 219.7 x 43.1 x 52 cm
The Dakis Joannou Collection

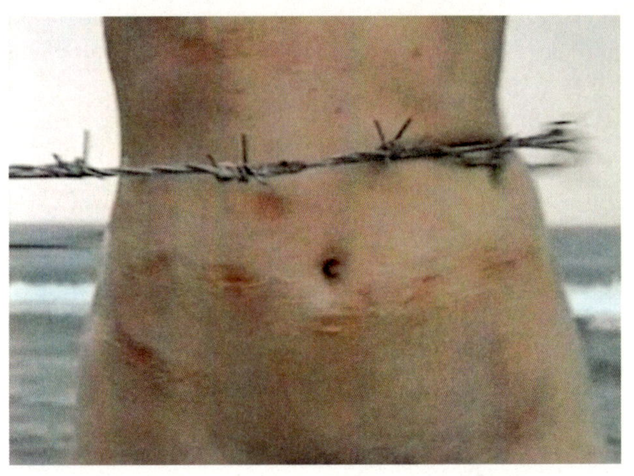

SIGALIT LANDAU
Born in 1969 in Jerusalem (Israel), she lives and works in Tel Aviv.

Sigalit Landau often uses her own body as a means of expression, as in the tradition of body art. In this case, however, the violent action performed on the body carries political and social connotations. In the video, a childhood toy, the Hula-hoop, becomes the instrument of a deadly ritual, a self-imposed torture. The action takes place on a beach in Tel Aviv, to the indifference of occasional passers-by. The barbed wire evokes the perpetual state of conflict that plagues this area. Barbed wire is an aggressive material used to establish and guard borders and restrict freedom of movement; at the same time it also serves as a protection against enemies. The naked body of the artist, subjected to a slow, and apparently endless process of abrasion caused by its own movement, raises upsetting questions about the responsibility of both victims and their torturers.

Barbed Hula, 2000
Video; color, sound; 2'
Collection Magasin 3 Stockholm Konsthall

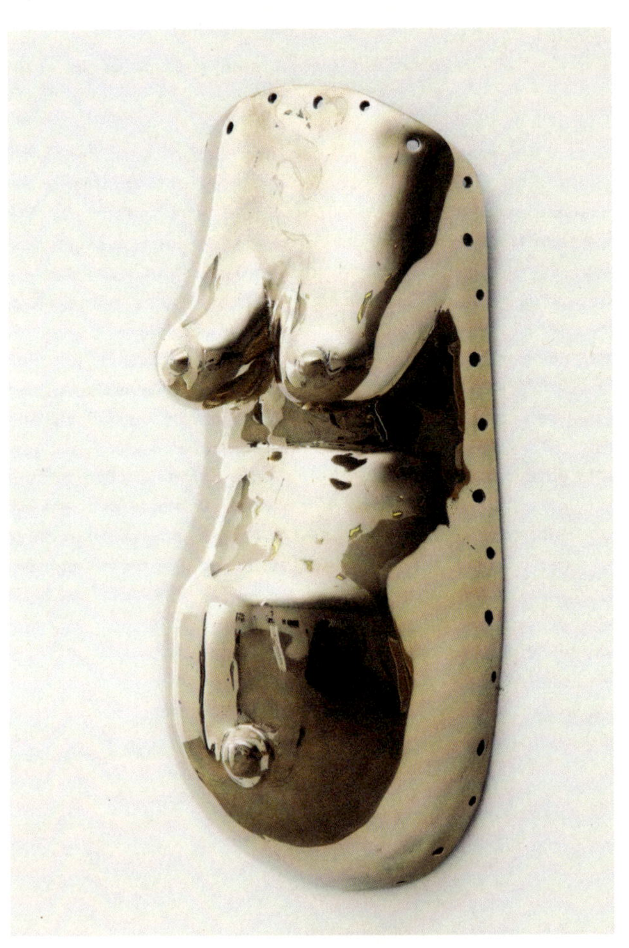

SHERRIE LEVINE
Born in 1947 in Hazleton (Pennsylvania, USA), she lives and works in New York.

Since the 1980s, Sherrie Levine has been regarded as one of the most representative women artists of so-called "appropriationism," an artistic practice that involves the critical re-use of images drawn from art history and the mass media. The act of appropriation aims at showing the extent to which the meaning of images is dependent on their use and the context of their exhibition.
Body Mask belongs to a recent series of polished bronze works derived from the ritual Makondo masks of south-eastern Tanzania. In their original cultural context, these masks depict the body of a pregnant woman, and are worn by men during initiation rites. Levine reproduces the masks in bronze and presents them as luxury goods, with the aim of questioning the relationship between the ritual use of the masks and their role as exhibited objects, and the different cultural meaning their reproduction acquires in each context.

Body Mask, 2007
Bronze sculpture; 57.2 x 24.1 x 14.6 cm
Collection Fondazione Sandretto Re Rebaudengo, Turin

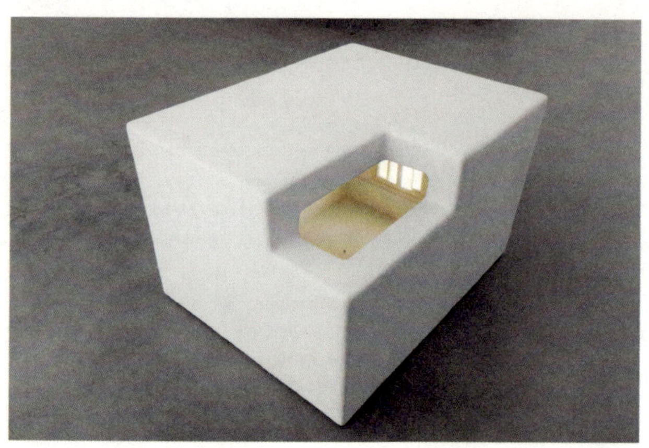

DEANNA MAGANIAS
Born in 1967 in Washington, DC (USA), she lives and works
in Athens.

DeAnna Maganias employs forms and materials that hark
back to modernism, reducing minimal volumes and surfaces
until they fit into the personal sphere. *The View From Bed*
focuses on the "point of view" as both a perceptual and
communicative tool. Architecture, in this case the interior
space of Maganias' bedroom, whose scale reproduction is
placed inside the cube that constitutes the sculpture and
rotated by 180° on the horizontal axis, becomes the pretext for a dizzying reversal of the public's point of view,
which comes to coincide with the artist's own, intimate perspective. The bed, whose volume is extracted from the cube
that delimits the room walls, thus permitting a view inside
it, becomes the missing link between two discordant views,
the hole of a camera obscura that reflects a disturbing
view of reality.

The View From Bed, 2007
Mixed media sculpture; 101 x 130 x 160 cm
The Dakis Joannou Collection

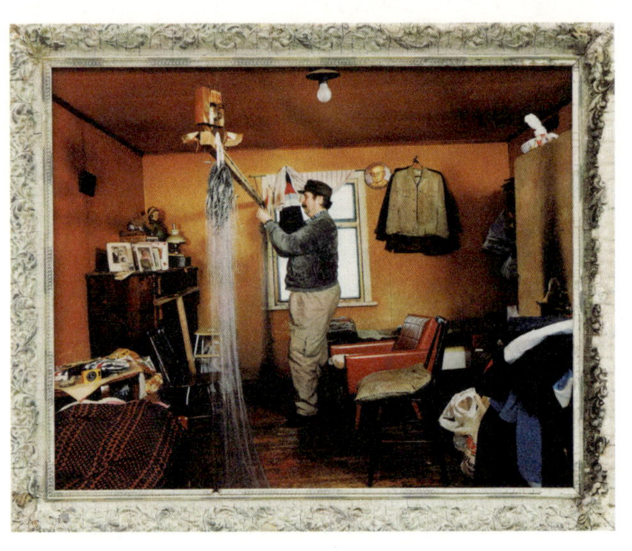

ESKO MÄNNIKKÖ

Born in 1959 in Pudasjärvi (Finland), he lives and works in Oulu (Finland).

Esko Männikkö works with photography as a social document. One of his main interests is portraying individuals in the environment they inhabit. His investigations focus on economically and geographically marginal situations, as in this series devoted to bachelors living in isolation in the north of Finland. The photographs were the result of a long process, during which the artist deepened his knowledge of the subjects and the context in which they live, developing a personal relationship with them. The rooms, furnishings, and clothes all contribute to build an image of the person represented. Although they seem staged, these images are very rarely manipulated. Instead these environments contribute to the image of the person represented. Yet each photograph is also a rigorous abstract composition and manages to reach a sophisticated synthesis between social content and aesthetic form.

Kittilä, 1995
C-print; 53 x 68 cm
Kuivaniemi, 1994
C-print; 57 x 63 cm
Kuivaniemi, 1993
C-print; 67 x 57.5 cm
← *Kuivaniemi*, 1993
C-print; 52.5 x 63 cm

Kuivaniemi, 1992
C-print; 40.5 x 48.5 cm
Hyrynsalmi, 1990
C-print; 61.5 x 51.5 cm
Hyrynsalmi, 1990
C-print; 71 x 61 cm
Utajärvi, 1990
C-print; 49.5 x 59.5 cm

Collection Magasin 3 Stockholm Konsthall

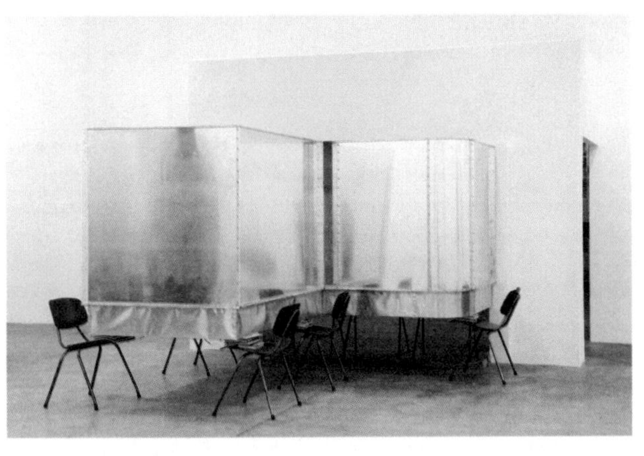

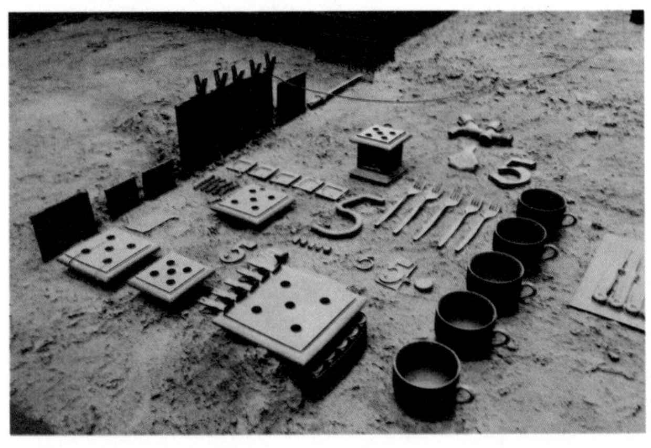

MARK MANDERS

Born in 1968 in Volkel (Netherlands), he lives and works in Arnhem (Netherlands) and Ronse (Belgium).

The work of Mark Manders, which the artist himself describes as a "self-portrait as a building," contrasts the rationality of architecture with the frailty of human existence. His sculptures and installations are suspended in a mysterious, dreamlike atmosphere. The scale reduction, often expressed as a percentage figure in the work's title, only adds to this effect of estrangement. *Nocturnal City Scene* is the model for a city made from found objects such as forks, tin cups, and other household implements. The work, a still life in black, is pervaded by a stifling atmosphere, a sinister omen of catastrophe that recalls the image of a necropolis. This work is a formal and conceptual response to Manders' own study of the similarities and differences between the—rationally impeccable—architectonic aspects of structure and the size of organic and totemic objects.

← *Nocturnal City Scene*, 1993
Installation; aluminum, sand, chairs, books, glass, rope;
290 x 350 x 200 cm
Top: installation view; bottom: detail of the interior
Collection Fondazione Sandretto Re Rebaudengo, Turin

Fragment from Self-Portrait as a Building/Room with Landscape with Fake Ballpoint, 1993
Mixed media, 141 x 482 x 220 cm
Collection Fondazione Sandretto Re Rebaudengo, Turin

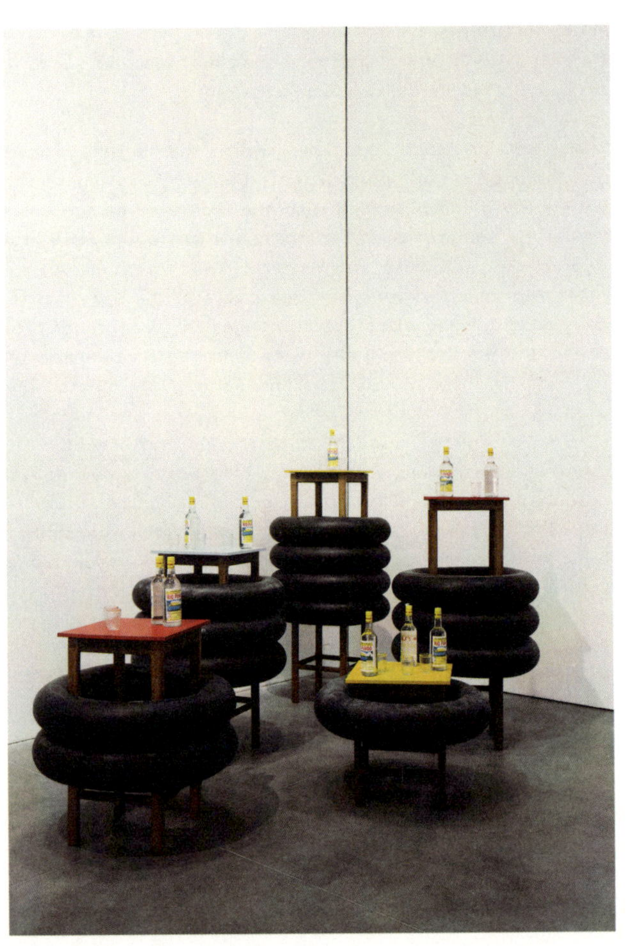

MAREPE

Born in 1970 in Santo Antonio de Jesus (Brazil), he lives
and works in Santo Antonio de Jesus.

Marepe's work belongs on the border area between utili-
tarianism and poetry. Everyday objects from his own living
environment are re-contextualized and charged with new
meaning. This practice recalls not only classic artistic
strategies such as the readymade, but also local customs.
Because the region of Bahia, in northeastern Brazil, is
peopled for the most part by the descendants of runaway
slaves, and is economically depressed, its inhabitants are
forced to use objects and materials inventively every day.
Rio Fundo (Deep River) is named after the Brazilian region
where cachaça is produced. Bottles of the alcohol stand
on small tables along with empty glasses—a common sight
in the bars and streets of this area. The artist hopes to
preserve this scene intact over time, by ironically fitting
the tables with air tubes, often used as life jackets by the
inhabitants of Bahia.

Rio Fundo, 2004
Installation; wood, rubber, glass, cachaça, formica;
variable dimensions
Ellipse Foundation – Contemporary Art Collection, Cascais

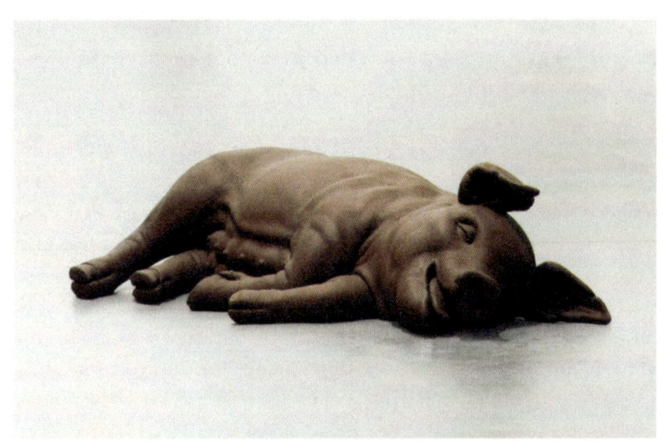

PAUL MCCARTHY
Born in 1945 in Salt Lake City (Utah, USA), he lives and
works in Altadena (California).

Paul McCarthy's works have often been referred to as
disconcerting, due to the artist's ability to analyze the
American imagination and its iconography, and distort both
until he reaches the "disturbing," i.e. the unsettling union
of what is known with what is altogether foreign. For example, McCarthy created a psychopath version of Santa
Claus, who turned the Christmas party into a repulsive
whirligig of fluids, found objects, blood, and dirt. The artist
then presented this very same icon in a plump, inflatable,
unthreatening version. The pig is a recurring subject in
McCarthy's work. In *Pig*, the animal, which generally carries
negative connotations, is cleaned up and turned into a
harmless, Disney-like character. It is lying on the ground, in
a strange condition of both peacefulness and suffering,
health and illness. This puts the spectator before a bizarre,
ambiguous being, half-way between human and animal.

Pig, 2003
Silicone rubber; 142 x 91 cm
The Dakis Joannou Collection

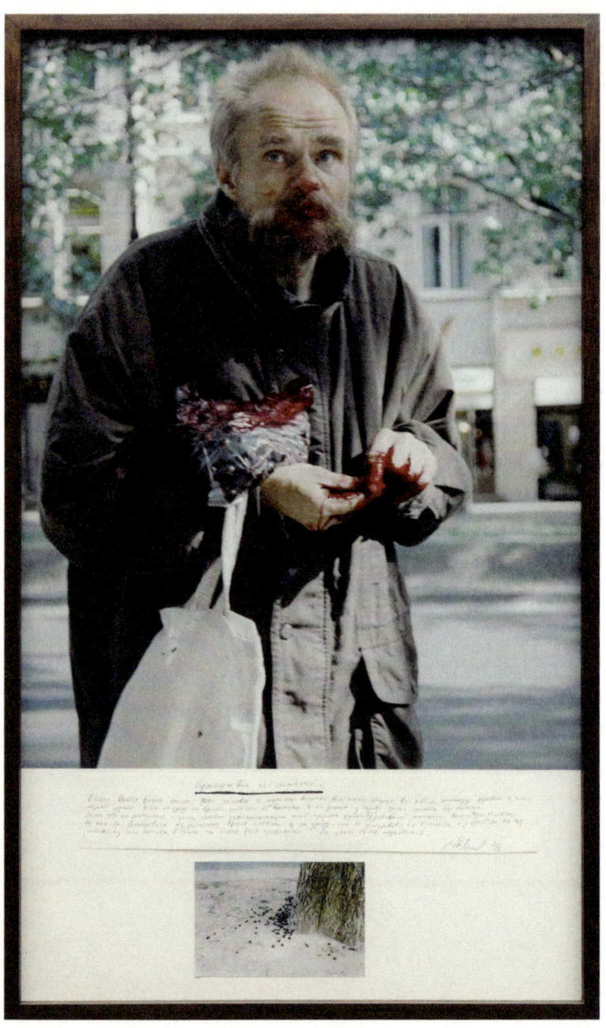

BORIS MIKHAILOV

Born in 1938 in Kharkov (Ukraine), he lives and works in Kharkov and Berlin.

Boris Mikhailov creates major photographic series exploring the individual's position within the public sphere of ideology, be it communist or capitalistic. The famous series *Case History* (1999) documents the social disintegration that followed the collapse of the Soviet Union, and especially its repercussions on living conditions. With the cycle *Look at Me I Look at Water*, Mikhailov continues, in terms both of themes and forms, his exploration of degraded humanity, physically and morally scarred by the loss of its identity. Taken during a long trip from East to West, these pictures are accompanied by short handwritten commentaries by the artist, which emphasize the feeling of finding oneself in front of a private photographic album.
But the humanity he portrays with fierce realism is one that is not familiar to us; it is on the contrary one that is almost invisible from the point of view of our comfortable lives. Mikhailov's work forces us to acknowledge these men and women and face their harsh existence.

Look at Me I Look at Water, 1999
C-print, handwriting; 87.5 x 52cm
Collection Antoine de Galbert, La maison rouge, Paris

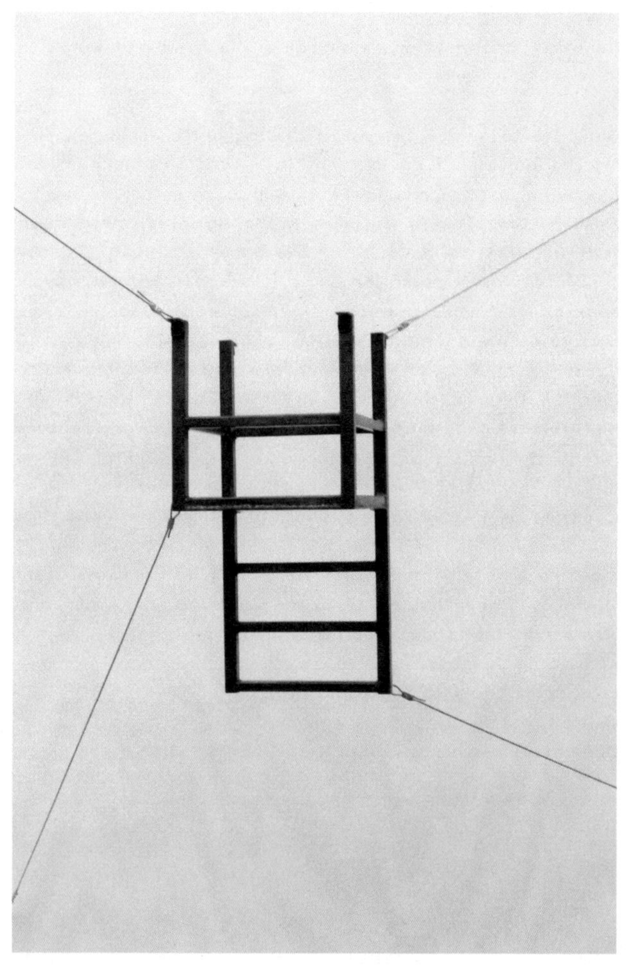

BRUCE NAUMAN
Born in 1941 in Fort Wayne (Indiana, USA), he lives and works in Galisteo (New Mexico).

Bruce Nauman is a key figure in the renewal of the language of art from a conceptual and performative perspective. Since the 1960s he has created works in the most diverse media, from video to installation, drawing to sculpture. During the 1980s, the linguistic experiments in his works started to exhibit a more overtly political content, such as in pieces inspired by South American dictatorial regimes and the practice of political torture. These works explore violence, cruelty, and a human condition dominated by fear. In *Untitled (Suspended Chair, Vertical III)*, the chair evokes those used in interrogations and capital executions, but also functions as a substitute for the human figure: made unserviceable as an instrument of torture, the chair is placed in an uncomfortable, frustrating position, and becomes itself a victim of torture.

Untitled (Suspended Chair, Vertical III), 1987
Installation; welded steel and steel cables;
variable dimensions
Collection Magasin 3 Stockholm Konsthall

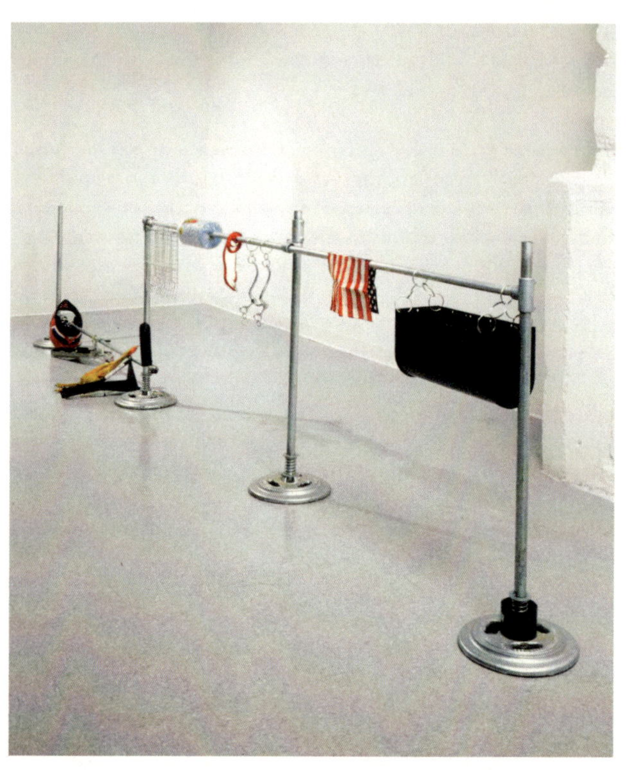

CADY NOLAND
Born in 1956 in Washington, DC (USA), she lives and works
in New York.

Cady Noland appropriates found objects and images of
famous people, with which she analyzes the stereotype of
the American dream and its crisis, which began in 1960 with
the Vietnam War and the student movement. Utilizing mur-
ders and political scandals from the media, Noland deals
with the failure of a utopian idea. In *Drag*, Noland's use of
metal bars, a recurring element in the artist's work, is
somewhat different. Used as gates and grids in other
works, the bars become an icon of the violence embraced by
the United States in its pursuit of independence and freedom. In time, this violent mentality has crept into the very
fabric of American society, spreading to the point of influ-
encing individual relationships. In *Drag*, however, Noland
leaves the work in a state of apparent incompleteness—
with the bars left open, the work suggests the possibility of
change.

Drag, 1990
Metal poles, helmet, and found objects; variable dimensions
The Dakis Joannou Collection

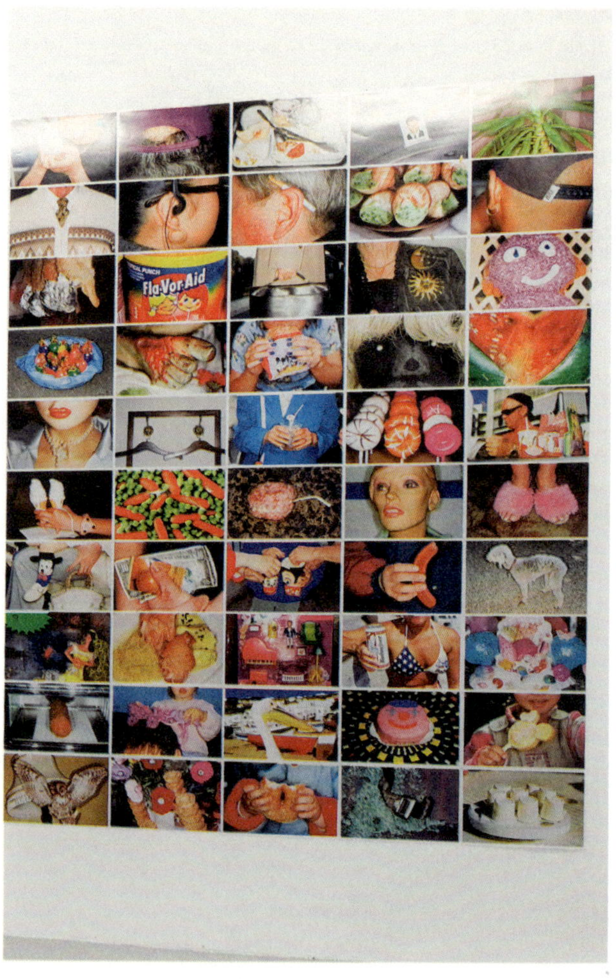

Fla-Vor-Aid

MARTIN PARR

Born in 1952 in Epsom (United Kingdom), he lives and works in Bristol.

Martin Parr's photographs cast a caustic, ironic glance at fragments of everyday life, portraying an existence at the mercy of excesses caused by abundance and the consumer habits of today's society. The pictures are taken and collected with the devotion of an ethnographer, and are exhibited like the documents of a long field research. In the portfolio *Common Sense*, a project begun in the mid-1990s, Parr brings together and exhibits a series of photographic details that range from sex toys to doughnuts to the kitsch bikinis worn by bizarre bathers. Through the use of close-up shots, Parr's photographs seem to annihilate individuality and leave room only for merchandise as a sign of a standardized collective identity. Unified by garish colors, the pictures point to the shared artificiality of consumer society.

Common Sense, 1999, detail
250 laser prints; 21 x 29.7 cm each
Collection Antoine de Galbert, La maison rouge, Paris

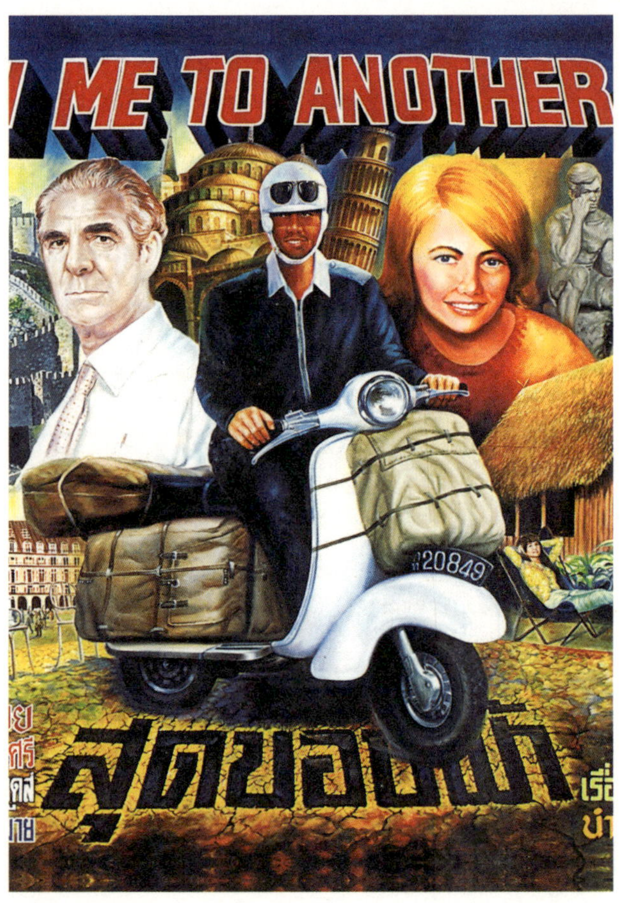

ME TO ANOTHER
20849

NAVIN RAWANCHAIKUL
Born in 1971 in Chiang Mai (Thailand), he lives and works in
Thailand and Japan.

Drawing inspiration from the widespread Thai custom of
painting billboards and commercial posters, Navin Rawanchaikul succeeds in erasing the line between art and traditional handmade production. His works are the expression
of an aesthetic of appropriation that involves cinema and
advertising imagery recast in new narrative contexts, functions, and interpretations. *Fly With Me To Another World
(Dedicated)* is a large acrylic-on-canvas painting that nar-
rates the almost mythological deeds of Inson Wongsman,
who, in 1962, embarked on a scooter trip from Thailand to
Italy. Traveling thus becomes a time for crossing borders
and countries, for exchanging and meeting. Places of
departure and destination are only the pretext for a narrative in which all hierarchies, both aesthetic and political,
are abolished.

Fly With Me To Another World (Dedicated), 1999, detail
Acrylic on canvas; 278 x 810 cm
Collection Fondazione Sandretto Re Rebaudengo, Turin

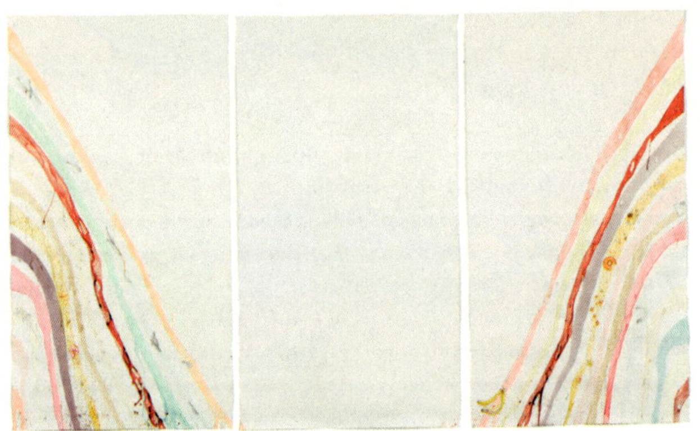

AUREL SCHMIDT
Born in 1982 in Kamloops (Canada), she lives and works in
New York.

In the drawings of Aurel Schmidt, urban waste of every kind
mixes with cockroaches and other insects, forming Arcim-
boldo-like compositions, described by the artist as gothic-
realism, due to the analytical style she uses to deal with
abject, upsetting themes. *So Damn Pure* belongs to a cycle
of works in which Schmidt appropriates masterpieces of
modern art history, in this case works by Morris Louis, and
completely defaces them by using repulsive materials.
Acrylic paint is 'enriched' with urine, spit, and blood, as well
as medicine, mouthwash, beer, and coffee. Natural and artificial waste products mingle in an apparently refined composition, an abstract image that soon reveals its link to
base reality.

So Damn Pure, 2008
Mixed media on paper (pencil, colored pencil, beer, blood,
Pepto-Bismol, wine, grape Crush, Imodium, coffee, Kool-Aid,
Listerine, Tang, urine, Comet, Sour Apple Daiquiri mix, spit,
acrylic); 267 x 421 x 5 cm
Collection Fondazione Sandretto Re Rebaudengo, Turin

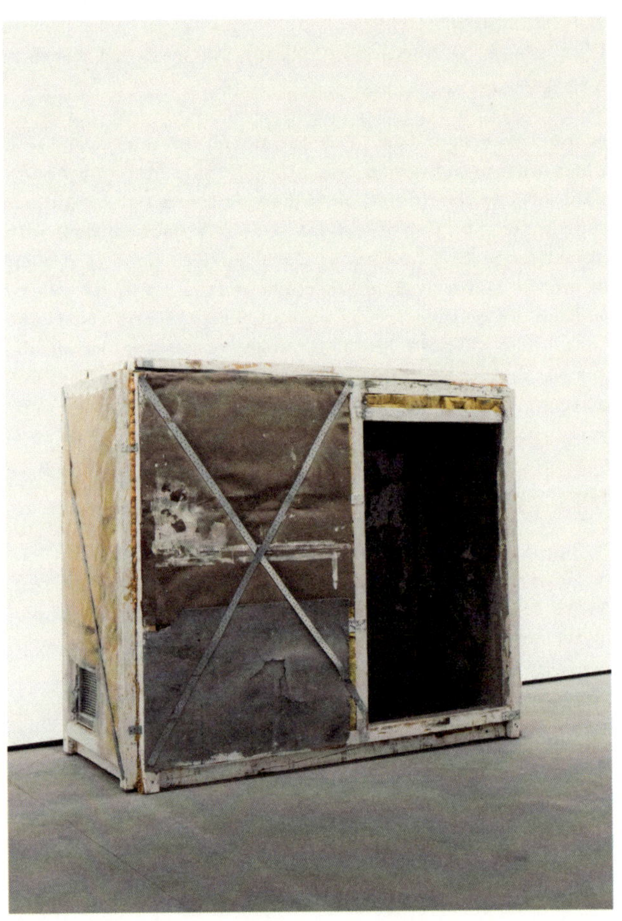

GREGOR SCHNEIDER

Born in 1969 in Rheydt (Germany), he lives and works in Rheydt.

Since the 1980s, Gregor Schneider has created installations that analyze the complex connections between physical space and individuality. His research has taken the form of a morbid relationship with the house where he has been living and working since the age of 16, and which the artist calls *Totes Haus u r* ("Dead house u r"). Over time, the building has become a constantly changing labyrinth in which rooms multiply or change place—the artist moves doors and windows, as in a horror film, so that the visitor loses his sense of orientation. *Das Große Wichsen* is one of the rooms in the house. The title, which translates as "the big jerk-off," reveals the true nature of the room, which, like the rest of the house, is not a comfortable, agreeable place, but the materialization of the artist's fears. Schneider manifests all his obsessions by endlessly rearranging a shelter for his own soul.

Das Große Wichsen, 1997
Mixed media installation; 264 x 124 x 244 cm
Collection Fondazione Sandretto Re Rebaudengo, Turin

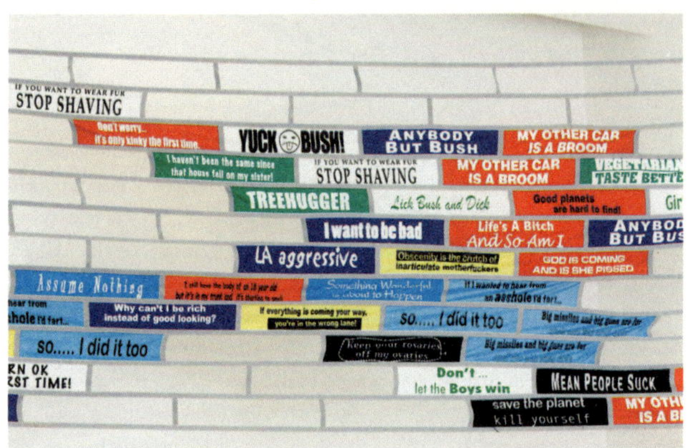
IF YOU WANT TO WEAR FUR
STOP SHAVING
Don't worry...
it's only kinky the first time.
YUCK BUSH!
ANYBODY BUT BUSH
MY OTHER CAR IS A BROOM
I haven't been the same since
that house fell on my sister!
IF YOU WANT TO WEAR FUR
STOP SHAVING
MY OTHER CAR IS A BROOM
VEGETARIANS TASTE BETTER
TREEHUGGER
Lick Bush and Dick
Good planets are hard to find!
Gir
I want to be bad
Life's A Bitch And So Am I
ANYBODY BUT BUS
LA aggressive
Obscenity is the crutch of inarticulate motherfuckers
GOD IS COMING AND IS SHE PISSED
Assume Nothing
I still have the body of an 18 year old
but it's in my trunk and it's starting to smell
Something Wonderful is about to Happen
If I wanted to hear from an asshole I'd fart...
hear from
hole I'd fart...
Why can't I be rich instead of good looking?
If everything is coming your way,
you're in the wrong lane!
so..... I did it too
Big missiles and big guns are for
so..... I did it too
Keep your rosaries off my ovaries
Big missiles and big guns are for
RN OK
RST TIME!
Don't...
let the Boys win
MEAN PEOPLE SUCK
save the planet
kill yourself
MY OTH
IS A B

LARA SCHNITGER

Born in 1969 in Harleem (Netherlands), she lives and works in Los Angeles.

Lara Schnitger's work turns fabric into the human figure or architecture, language becomes image, and poetry is charged with political meaning. The artist employs "humble" materials and handcraft techniques such as sewing to create installations and sculptures that cast an ironic look on today's society. *Gridlock* is an imposing installation that brings together elements belonging to different epochs, places, and cultures that the artist herself has come across during her many travels. The structure is inspired by the safety fencing of Japanese building sites, but is intertwined with Tibetan prayer flags and windshield stickers of the kind you often come across in the US, especially during electoral campaigns. Prayers, political slogans, irreverent messages, are all blended in a patchwork that evokes both cultural diversity and the universal way we express desire.

Gridlock, 2005, detail
Installation; cotton, ribbon; variable dimensions
Collection Magasin 3 Stockholm Konsthall

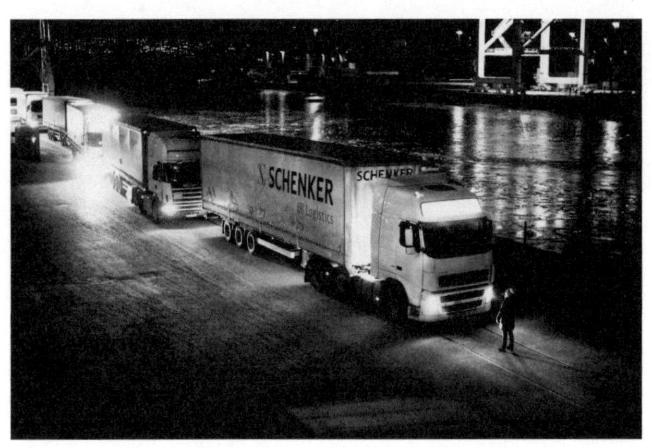

SANTIAGO SIERRA
Born in 1966 in Madrid (Spain), he lives and works in Lucca
(Italy).

Since the 1990s Santiago Sierra has worked on creating
critical actions that analyze the conventions and con-
straints of the social, economic, and political system. He
has created highly controversial performances and installations using direct and sometimes violent tactics to deal
with the individual's position in relation to power systems.
PERSON OBSTRUCTING A LINE OF CONTAINERS is the video
documention of a performance that took place in the port
area of Stockholm. The action is very simple but has a
strong emotional impact, and makes use of a recurring
strategy in Sierra's work, that is, the creation of an obsta-
cle, a barrier that interrupts or subverts the normal
functioning of a device. Here the artist focuses on trans-
portation and the exchange of goods, which, in a capitalist
system, paradoxically enjoy greater freedom of movement
than people.

PERSON OBSTRUCTING A LINE OF CONTAINERS,
Kaj 3 Frihamnen, Stockholm, Sweden, 2009
Video; black & white, sound; 10'
Collection Magasin 3 Stockholm Konsthall

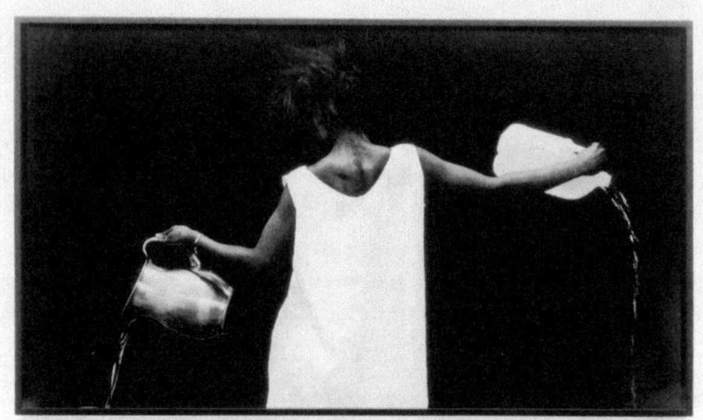

SHE SAW HIM DISAPPEAR BY THE RIVER,
THEY ASKED HER TO TELL WHAT HAPPENED,
ONLY TO DISCOUNT HER MEMORY.

LORNA SIMPSON
Born in 1960 in Brooklyn (New York, USA), she lives and works in Brooklyn.

Lorna Simpson explores racial and gender issues through language that blends her past as a documentary photographer with a conceptual use of the photographic medium. In *Water Bearer*, the immediate reading of the image is complicated by a written comment that encourages us to view history as a cultural text that can unearth repressed or forgotten memories, but does not grant equal opportunities to all subjects to speak. In *Myths*, the combination of diverse elements and the scientific aesthetic alludes to the oppressive act of cataloging people according to pre-determined classes or groups. *Untitled (Cabin in the Sky)* examines the construction of the "black" stereotype in history, literature, and other creative forms of expression.

← *Water Bearer*, 1986
Gelatin silver print with vinyl lettering; 114 × 195 cm
Ellipse Foundation – Contemporary Art Collection, Cascais

Myths, 1991
Gelatin silver prints with engraved plastic plaques;
109 × 363 cm
Ellipse Foundation – Contemporary Art Collection, Cascais

Untitled (Cabin in the Sky), 2001
Gelatin silver prints, plexiglas, vinyl; 154.9 × 104.1 cm
Ellipse Foundation – Contemporary Art Collection, Cascais

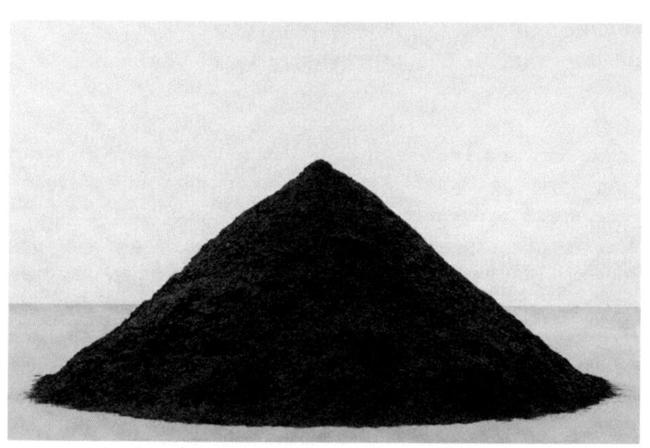

STÉPHANE THIDET
Born in 1974 in Paris (France), he lives and works in Paris.

In Stéphane Thidet's works, ordinary objects and materials are employed to create distorted visions of reality, imaginary worlds that look like dreams or nightmares. The artist deprives the objects of their original functions and transforms them, or moves them to new, ambiguous situations. *Sans titre (Le Terril)* consists of a black monumental heap that recalls one of the many coal deposits that covered the landscape of northern France until the collapse of the mine industry in the 1970s. On closer inspection, the heap turns out to be made of tons of black confetti, a material with very different connotations—that of festive celebrations. In Thidet's installation, the accumulation becomes ephemeral and transitory because of the very lightness of the material employed. The apparently stable, threatening form is actually liable to change with the slightest current of air.

Sans titre (Le Terril), 2008
Installation; 2 tons of black confetti; diameter: 5 m, height: 2.5 m
Collection Antoine de Galbert, La maison rouge, Paris

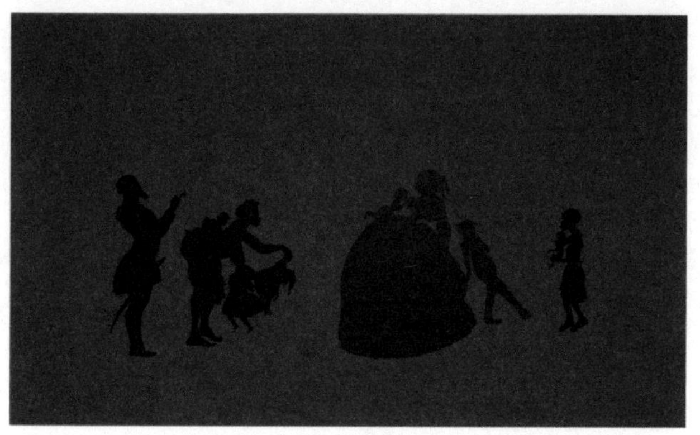

KARA WALKER
Born in 1969 in Stockton (California, USA), she lives and
works in New York.

Gender, race, and violence are the issues tackled in Kara
Walker's works. By cutting out silhouettes and applying
them to the walls of the exhibition space, the artist creates
bizarre, shocking, panoramic scenes, the characters of
which are stereotypical in terms of both their attitude and
physical features. Walker's figurines stand out as shadows
of pre-cinematic shows that tell us about a past world: the
dawn of America, when the history of the African-American
community started developing. The images are apparently
essential, barely outlined, yet on closer inspection they are
full of details and narrative hints, often terrifying, such as
stories of power abuse and violence. In a provocative
recasting of the "minstrel shows," a form of street enter-
tainment popular in the 19th century that offered a conventional, offensive image of black people, the artist
opens her space to a reflection on contemporary African-
American identity.

Untitled, 2005
Cut paper and adhesive on painted wall; variable dimensions
Ellipse Foundation – Contemporary Art Collection, Cascais

The Two Rooms

Aristide Antonas

I am tired, but it doesn't matter, I'll knock on the door though it's late. I don't care, I am too tired, can't be nice anymore. This door just happened to be there, because that's exactly what I was looking for, the door to the metal box. I have no idea who makes the metal boxes. But here's one, so I'll knock, late as it may be.

Who's there?

I am out of breath. Perhaps my tongue is sticking out a bit. I have to tell you something. I may have surprised you. But you must let me in. You will know once I show you what's in the bag.

I don't know you, sir. I can't let a stranger in.

Yes, you can if I just tell you something.

Tell me what?

You will know right away that I am no stranger, comes the soft growl from deep inside my throat.

Do I know you?

I don't think so.

Then you're a stranger.

No, I believe I am a stranger to nobody.

What will you tell me? What should I expect? I am peaceful now and the night is falling. What's there in that bag of yours?

I'll show you if you let me in. There's something I should tell you if only you'd let me.

I can't do that.

Then I'll go. I was tired and happened to see this door.

I thought I'd knock.
Is it some gift you will give to me?
If you like.
But what can it be? What could you give me?
Whatever you like from what's in the bag.
The door man stops to consider this.
Well, come in then. Just for a minute. You may sit at the table.
Thank you.
Well?
Well what?
Won't you speak then? Won't you show me what you've got there?
Oh, yeah, right, I will, absolutely, but first could you please get me some bread?
The door man gives an impatient snort.
Alright, I will. Hold on.
He gets up. No, I am not at all hungry. This chair is comfortable. The wind is blowing in through the window. The man returns with some bread and cheese in a plate.
I would very much like to know what you have to tell me and I would also like to see what's in the bag without any further delay.
Absolutely. You are very right to be impatient. But may I just have some bread first?
Please do.
I see his hands, that look like mine. They are hairy with crooked fingernails. His face is furrowed like mine. He is watching me.
In the meantime—I say, already munching at some bread—I could perhaps explain our special situation here. So, mainly, what I want to talk to you about concerns the bridge. The bridge is there as you can see and now it's time for the door. You are the door man. And which is the door would you say?

I raise my brow and give him an enigmatic look while still eating quietly.

Bridge, you say? The door situation? I have no idea what you're talking about. You'll have to explain, he says.

This is smoked cheese, isn't it? I ask, somewhat surprised.

Yes, it is.

I nod in appreciation as if to commend his particular choice of cheese. Then I start speaking slowly in a low voice, enunciating each word with a sense of gravity appropriate to the situation at hand.

The door I am referring to is your door. Because there is of course a matter that concerns others around here, around your neighborhood, your street, the whole district, perhaps now even your door and window. Are you aware of it?

No I am not, or maybe I am. What matter is that?

People are being rounded up and tied down to furniture. Someone is going around the houses here knocking on doors. Metal bridges like boxes are being built between the houses. Haven't you heard?

No, I haven't.

I nod again affirmatively and go on chewing slowly, because I am not really hungry.

Around the entire Resort, or just here?

I offer no answer to this question.

Well, you know, I was tired of walking—I pause to clear my throat and then I continue—and thought it was just as well, I'd knock on the door; it was late of course but, you see, I was exhausted, I just could not be nice anymore. Your door just happened to be there before me because I was looking for a brother behind the door.

The man takes the plate from me.

Is there something you'd like to say, something you'd like to give me? I asked for nothing. Who is going around the neighborhood knocking on our doors? Is it you? You promised a gift. What have you got there?

I open up the bag and look straight into his eyes as if try-
ing to hypnotize him. I show him the straps.
Here, for example, take a look at these.
What are they?
He is staring at the straps looking almost mesmerized, not
moving an inch in his chair.
Hold your arm still. There. Now the other one. See?
We're good. Now the leg. That's right. And the other one.
Great.
Now let me open the door.
I whistle loudly and a group of brothers that look like us
appear at the doorway. They always follow me from a dis-
tance. They'll show themselves only if I whistle. Once more
they obey in silence as I point to the armchairs and chairs
in the living room. I tie them down, each to a different seat.
Give me your name, I ask our host.
No.
As you wish. Now, pay attention my dear sir, I say as I pace
up and down the center of the room. I will leave you alone
with them for a while until you get to know each other. It is
important that you get to know each other so you can coor-
dinate. You are already a team of six.
Right, says the door man.
Something bad is going to happen in the house next door a
few days from now and I am going to tell you all about it in a
while.

Could these perhaps not be dogs? F. K.

It is even later now, time has flown by, but I just couldn't
give a damn. I am even more tired than before so I could
care even less about being nice. Before me stands the door
of the adjoining house. I have come out of one door and am
knocking on the next. I don't even have the strength to
speak. I am all played out.

Who is it?

I bend down and stoop to the ground.

There is something I must tell you, I manage to say under my breath with whatever little strength I have left. I may have surprised you, but I must come in and talk to you. You will know why once I show you what's in the bag.

I don't know you, sir. I can't just let you in. You are aware of what's been going on around people's houses these days.

You *can* let me in if I show you what's in the bag.

What's that?

You will know I am not a stranger.

But what can you tell me? What should I expect?

You will hear about things that have already happened and about things that are about to happen. You will also see some things.

What things?

Things that have to do with a project being carried out in the area.

Come in.

I see that the man who answered the door is not alone. Four more are with him, seated in the living room. They all have white, smooth, hairless skin. They are plump—three more men then, and a woman.

I stand despite being exhausted.

What are you doing here? asks the biggest of them all as though he were the leader of the group.

You must have seen the tunneled bridge that was attached here. Have you seen it? It begins at your house and leads to that of your neighbors. Have you noticed?

Yes, we have, answers the woman.

What? asks one of the fat men.

A bridge like a metal box, explains the woman.

It connects the house with the one next door, I add. Actually, this window is connected with one of the windows in the house next door. I pull up a stool, open the window, climb on the stool and show them how they can crawl through the window onto the tunneled bridge. Nobody moves.

Is it strong enough? asks again the fattest man. Can the structure support our weight? Assuming we'd want to cross it, that is?

Yes, it is supported by metal trusses planted into the ground.

Alright.

And now I will open the bag. I promised I would and will go right ahead without a moment's delay.

I leave the remaining straps aside and take out five knives all at once. I place one in front of each person sitting in the living room.

You can have a knife each. They are big and sharp.

The woman gives the man sitting next to her a knowing look. She was holding his hand and now she lets go to grab the metal object that is hers to take. She examines it from up close and then places it back on the table.

That's how things are.

As you can see, I am covered in black hair, my face is furrowed and my fingernails are crooked. I will return next door because my brothers are there. I just need one of you to escort me.

I'll go, says the woman. Maybe you'll go with me? she adds turning to the man next to her.

OK.

They wanted
to see me stray
from my path.
They failed.
If anything, they
achieved the
opposite.
My ability to stay
alert
was sharpened.
F. K.

It is almost dawn. We exit through the door and walk to the one next to it. I had left it open.

See? I am back as promised. Here are two neighbors from

the house next door. They were kind enough to escort me.

How do you do?

How do you do?

Glad to meet you.

Now, you have to tie me down as well to this remaining chair.

There are some straps left in the bag.

Alright, if you say so. We, for our part, promise to take care of your meals.

The machine is not social unless broken down to its constituent parts, themselves constituting a machine each in turn. G. D./F. G.

What misfortune occurred in the house next door?

They are all armed with knives and we are tied down.

If these dogs had asked me then what I thought of their conduct, I would perhaps have said that I approved of it. F. K.

I am woken up by a sound, a buzz coming from the window to the bridge. The window breaks open. The fattest of the men is now standing in the living room. He has tested the bridge's resilience to his weight. He is holding the knife. My brothers, the living room prisoners, are looking at him with puzzled eyes.

What's going on? I ask.

You can hear everything we say, can't you?

No, we can't.

What about this one here, sitting so close to the window? I bet he can hear.

No, he can't.

He walks up to the man sitting closer to the window.

So you can't hear, can you?

He cuts off his ear; places it upon the small table.

This will teach you not to lie and not to forget that you must not eavesdrop.

I thought it was a sound agreement, I say. But this could not have been foreseen. Some people will just break the rules. When we walk, we take a step with the right foot and then one with the left, but some people think they can change the way we walk. Now is the beginning of time without steps. The question is how to create time without steps. For there can be no revenge without time.

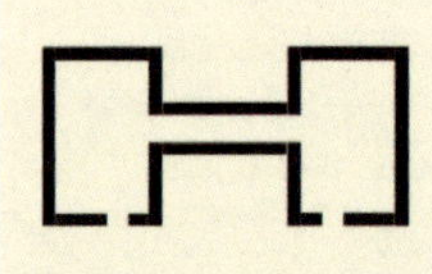

The woman comes in through the window. She is naked from the waist down. Her knife is held in a curious sheath that looks like a choker.

Have you had anything to eat? she asks. Don't look. Close your eyes.

We ignore her and she doesn't seem to care.

She tears at the clothes of a brother with her knife and then pulls at them and rips them off.

She gives him a hard-on and then sits on him.

There's nothing metaphorical about animalization. There's no symbolism or allegory implied in it. G. D./F. G.

You tied all of us down and then went and gave them knives?

Yes.

And then?

Then I asked them to tie me down too.

That was a mistake.
Let's sing, all together.
We will overcome baby,
We will overcome one day.
We are singing at the top of our voices. The walls are creak-
ing.
I see two shadows at the window; two neighbors holding
knives.
We stop singing. The neighbors leap down into the living
room.
Look at you bound like this; you are pathetic.
Why are you being loud?
Whose idea was it that got you tied down?
Won't anybody speak?
Who tied you down?
You don't need to know, replies the man whose ear has been
cut off.
Tell us who did it otherwise we'll kill this brother of yours
right here.
There is no answer.
One of the neighbors stabs the brother he had pointed at
in the stomach repeatedly.
Now will you tell us?
No.
He kills another.

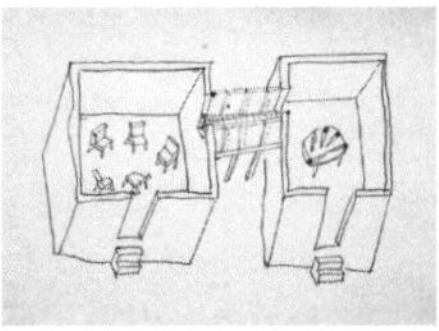

Summer is here. It is hot. Everyday they come to bring us a
dish of boiled chicken and rice. They feed us one by one. It
takes time. If you are hungry, you want to eat; the glands in
your mouth feel sore. If you eat, you feel sick. The food

smells bad. When lunch is over, they shove half a peach in
our mouths.

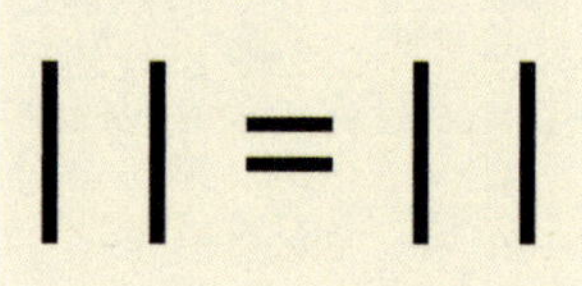

From inside the bridge comes the sound of steps again: two
neighbors we haven't seen here before. They walk up to us
and say: we have come to free you. This whole affair is over.
They release us cutting the straps with their knives and
look at us as if they loved us. But now my brothers take
hold of the knives and turn on them, stabbing them to
death. They cut off their heads and hang them at the window so they can be seen from across the bridge. The door
man is ready to abandon his house.
We go out into the street. Every step is hard—we have forgotten how to walk. We take one step with the right foot and
then one with the left. We go by the summer houses and
reach the shore. I am still holding the bag. I open it up.
There is still a strap and a knife in it. The bag is warm like
the body of an animal that has just died. I take out the
strap and wrap it around my waist like a belt. I secure the
knife on it. It feels safely in place against my waist. Without
holding anything in my hands I have it all. Perhaps I am no
longer an animal.
Have a good road ahead, I say to the door man.
He points to his own knife, the one he took from our deliver-
ers. He's already slipped it in his belt.
We should have killed you along with the others, he says. So
you owe us your life.

Translated from the Greek by Maria Skamaga.
The original title of this short story is Τα δύο δωμάτια.

Animal Stomach

Rui Cardoso Martins

I have an idea hanging from my head. It's been out there for ages. Everything suggests it's a bad idea.

My father handled unexpected problems much better, like on the day when he kicked down the olive trees. He had one hundred olive trees, one hundred years old, as he liked to put it, in a fondness for large numbers which speak of prosperity and abundance; however, once, when I arrived from my travels, he started digging the soil with the tip of his boot, detective-like, and, next to a dried ploughed earth, discovered a hole in the ground and called for the dog.

"Fetch, Tango!" my father shouted, but the dog was apathetic and never even showed up.

A dig elevated as a small volcano, it was a molehill, anthills are much more granular around the edges.
He picked out the closest olive tree and put his arms around it as if he hadn't seen it in years, until I felt moved by jealousy, after all, I had just arrived home from far abroad and he hadn't embraced me that way; however, all of a sudden, he began listening to its entrails, squeezing it, or smothering it, until he let go of it, tottering.

That evening, he had already inspected the grounds, from the house to the brook where the big water hemlock grows in mid-stream, which is to say, he checked tree after tree, clod by clod, and, snapping his tongue in an amusing sound, he announced his failure because all the century old roots of the one hundred olive trees were completely, and in his own words, nibbled away by those rats.

The master root, which should lay embedded underground, in the center, had vanished. Only some side roots, grazing on water and easily available nutrients, not buried more than ten inches deep where the soil is richer, the surface roots. The trees were going to die, if not now, soon. How did that happen?

He sat in the shade, stuck a finger underneath his cap and scratched his thinking spot. He did the maths, calculating the production costs, or pondering the suffering caused to trees, that were very dear to him—even though he hadn't planted them, he had taken care of them as family —their sap all dried up until no more olives sprang from the branches, those olive oil green eggs, the basis of our food regime, by the way. At bedtime, he had already decided on what to do.

For me, it's never this easy. I take loads of time even to pack a suitcase. By the time the sun reached the valley, from the east, and touched the tiny dewdrops that covered the grass like a blinking blanket, he was already kicking down olive trees.

He didn't know the first thing about martial arts, but he had a brawny body and his was a fighting spirit, I'm not quite sure if the more adequate one—self-defense, control, mediation, etc.—but a practical one, nonetheless, for instance: his brother, who was therefore my uncle, when he was young, split in half a gipsy who attacked him with his razor, using only a bludgeon that just so happened to belong to the gipsy. Something quite strong runs in this family's veins, maybe pride tempered with respect, which I hope I've inherited, evidently displayed in the olive trees knockdown, by passing over the Japanese tractor—the Kubota, always so useful in most chores, never left the storehouse on this particular occasion—and choosing the use of the direct kick, harder to execute.

He touched a tree with his index finger.

"Your turn, old girl, so sorry."

and stroke three blows, each time harder, four or five kicks sometimes, till the olive tree gave in; but he soon changed his method because at that rate he'd never make it, and so, later in that afternoon, he was seen dashing through the air, delivering high impact kicks, knocking the trunk at once, laughing like a bird, without ever losing his poise in those calf skin still-toe boots, his brow all sweaty

"Where to now, you rats?"

intending to scare them before the eviction, the remainder of the mission, we were soon to discover. By sundown, the last olive tree awaited. It hanged on as much as it could, but it too fell, its roots pulled out, chewed up arteries of the neck. Now, it was a dying field of horizontal trees with a house out in the back, unguarded. And the old man sat on the floor with the logs and wept for a while.

Adjust to the world's mess. Be flexible, elastic. Maybe my father would know what to do now; if only he had kicked my skull at the right moment, perhaps the meaning of things, the pleasure and the joy, which are so dear to me, would still be in my heart, controlling everything, instead of this unpleasant idea, hanging from my head. My dad kicked down those trees because he had a plan.

A fine plan.

Next week, we lumbered the trees, and the leaves and the small branches were burned in the center of the field, a blue smoke rising up to the sky. The larger chunks, sawed with the Black & Decker, were aligned on a stack next to the stone wall, which duplicated, as it were, the wooden wall that provided for firewood many years on, in spite of its being hollow and bitten by the beasts. Not just moles but all kinds of insects, cicadas, ants, crickets, as well as woodpeckers foraging for insects. Over there, there are also nightingales, thrushes, starlings, goldfinches, brown jays, turtledoves, partridges and, of course, sparrows, which almost don't count at all because they're everywhere on Earth, excepting the poles, so I have noticed on my travels. Sparrows are pretty much like sardines, only sardines, so they say, can be grilled even in the poles. Sparrows are best when fried, crunchy birdies.

In the summer, the countryside's blaring reaches the skies: imagine a thousand cell phones and fax machines and videogames booming their music all at once.

In our house, we almost never spent any firewood, even in the peak of winter. My father was old school: sleeping with open windows is good for you, it airs the lungs with cool oxygen, weak chests included, which did away with my mother quite early, by the way.

Nevertheless, the autopsy we performed on the olive trees revealed that the first diagnosis was correct, the trees were living-dead: people who can handle the unexpected properly are able to see all of the problem's dimensions, from its birth until the day it harms us.

Then, we did the glass sowing.

Before that, however, we placed one bottle marking every single mole hole, or every small mound that resembled a gallery, and signaled where it branched out. Under the slope that could be covered in a two-minute run, from the house's front door to the valley where the larger hemlock grows—racing up would take a four-minute run, though—we could cover the entire grounds from any vantage-point there: in that two acre square of old olive trees there was a large subterranean city of moles and other rodents. Generations acquiring a great knowledge of the soil, feeding on worms and maggots and, of course, the tender master roots serving as its basis, in a quite unique and balanced habitat. The dog gave us a little help

"Fetch, Tango, fetch!"

but it wasn't the old Tango anymore, so it took its

time doing its sniffing—that is, if it was indeed making any use of its precious snout: its sense of smell seemed to be in some sort of auto-mode, without the thrill, the speed and the accuracy of before.

A few weeks later, the dog disappeared. Either it got hit by a car—addicted as it was to throwing itself onto the road, to snap at tires—and fell into a ditch, where it rotted away and ended up being eaten, or it got poisoned by our neighbor and was secretly buried.

The neighbor never forgave that one of his sheep was bitten to death, and always wrongly blamed Tango and its mountain-dog friends for it. I don't know about the other dogs, but I'm pretty sure Tango didn't do it, being such an animal lover as Tango was, a very humane dog in my opinion, sometimes it almost seemed that it could speak to us, and it never even mind when the cats and the rabbits stole all the pellets from its bowl!

When Tango disappeared, we searched, searched, we yelled, yelled, we whistled, whistled and one morning when my father met the neighbor on the road carrying a bucket full of fresh figs, he asked him bluntly

"Good day, neighbor, were you the one who killed my dog?"

"It wasn't me, neighbor. But if you must know, I'm not the least bit sad about it, 'cause I really loved Ophelia, the little lamb."

Regardless, back in the afternoon when we used the bottles to pinpoint the mole's positions, everything was still just fine between us, and the neighbor showed up unexpectedly and offered his muscular assistance in return for a nice pitcher of pomace brandy to snuggle away in his fridge: he negotiated merrily, sticking out a few cork fingers to demonstrate the required amount and my father agreed.

It is likely Tango already suffered from Alzheimer's

back in those days, it's very likely ... That's why it didn't immediately respond when called, that's why it couldn't remember its own name all of a sudden, nor its master's face and voice, or what it had done the day before, or what it had just barked a couple of minutes ago, and neither, this being so, its role in society as a guard—both of the house and of the lands—and as our faithful friend.

Therefore, incidentally, how could it have throttled Ophelia suffering from such a condition? Unless Alzheimer's made it think it was a wolf, like the one's that once thrived in these mountains, or that it was a person ... Who knows? Maybe it decided it should start mimicking our killing methods, is that it? Oh, come on, neighbor, don't be ridiculous!

I only hope that when Tango disappeared, knowing so little of the world—since it never traveled seeking knowledge as I have, except for those couple of days when it would go to hills, looking for bitches, and from which it always returned skinny, filthy and shaky, its tongue steaming—again, I just hope it didn't yelp, filled with nostalgia and hurting for us, who fed it and cherished it more than any other creature it ever came across, including the bitches, by the way.

To be honest, I too have wasted a lot of love on my travels—until I was left with very little—and it very well may be that no one ever loved me quite as much as that dog did.

I suggested we went to the brook to get some hemlock for the moles but my dad cautioned against it, seeing that these pests, and all rodents as a matter of fact, are able to sniffle like crazy, with their tiny little rosy snout. So, it would never be as it is with sheep and cows that die because they mistake the hemlock leaves for parsley and the hemlock roots for wild carrots or for parsnip, because it's all so similar. Once they eat it, nothing refluxes for them to ruminate, like it happens with straw, which comes back up to be chewed over and over again, until finally it is digested in the four stomach compartments and enters the bloodstream, calorie-sized. Water hemlock works fast, the tongue rolls over itself, they get a nervous look, they start foaming from their mouths and when their lungs paralyze, it's bye, bye, cow.

The same thing can happen to a person, and such cases have indeed been reported: some people go to the cork oak forests to pick mushrooms, they make a mistake, from which make a stew, and then the entire family goes straight to the cemetery or to the top of the national list for liver transfusions. In this place, those who like to die usually use a hanging-rope round a cork oak branch, or use the jump into a water well, or the classic E-605 Strong, a poison against potato beetles which can be purchased in any drugstore in town.

Instead of any of these, to do away the moles, my dad placed his absolute trust on the glass method. He had learned it from a TV documentary about gardens in Europe. How Belgians, for example, exterminate the moles that ruin their wonderful back-lawns. We shouldn't be afraid of using whatever works abroad, he said, I don't know why you travel so much if you don't learn any useful stuff.

I even got the unpleasant feeling that all he knew about moles, about their lifestyle, their nourishment, about how they reproduce, etc., was not something his father taught him, passed on by his father's father, my great grandfather—far from it, I suspect it was all picked up in a single afternoon, watching TV. I could be wrong, though.

Anyhow, the procedure was simply unheard of in our neck of the woods. At the agreed time, we grabbed a few stones and we began to smash bottles into little shards. A contemporary piece, like the ones that play on the radio, a concert of broken glass, celebrated with a yell or a whistle every time a certain type of bottle, or the nature of the swing, its angle, etc, would produce sharp edged shards, cutting and pointy. Green glass bottles, for wine, favored this occurrence much more than the beer ones, brown colored, which tend to get round edged when they shatter.

We then poked the fragments deep into the ground, over the little mole houses, in every door and every window of each burrow. Wearing gloves, we threw the content of the polyester bag into the air, good old-fashioned handfuls, as if we were sowing shards. The provisions were short so I went to the supermarket riding my Famel Zundapp, and brought back a bag of wine bottles on it reinh, neihn, neihn, nhein, nhein, which required some serious drinking before we smashed them and scattered their glass seeds. And so, we ended the day with our hands in our pockets, singing a rather comical song our neighbor taught us, of which I can no longer remember neither the name, nor the sense, nor the tune.

But I do remember my dad talking to last bottle:

"Now, I'm gonna plant grapevines here and make some wine."

A few days after the shard sowing, a fingernail stump emerged, with a bit of blood and of flesh attached to it, carried by ants. We dug the spot with a hoe and there it was, the first casualty. The mole had cut its finger, its claw, or whatever the tip of the paw is called, which the animal uses for excavating galleries, in a continuous and curious motion as if it was swimming breaststroke inside the earth, pushing the rubble aside. That removed soil must go some place, hence the surface mounds.

With a cut paw, it is impossible.

We unearthed it and saw its pink nose turned upwards, its two huge teeth gripping the lower jaw. In those two little dots of blinded eyes, closed, there was disillusionment for having met its death in the dark, injured, thirsty and famished. Every single day of that week other cases surfaced, even families in some instances, which we unearthed and then buried again in a common grave, near the leafiest of chestnut-trees, and called it the mole cemetery.

All these proceedings, so necessary to our agriculture, proved detrimental to both my health and my state of mind, as very well could happen to any one with real feelings. Nonetheless, it was around that time that I enjoyed the grandest meal of my entire life. I ate from lunchtime till late in the evening and ended up discussing, with several peo-ple, that unpleasant mole business ...

… and one other matter, much worse ...

… maybe the combined effect of things … it was only since then, I must admit it … that sensation in my stom-ach, that tiny animal shaking … all the weight on just one side of my head … the appetite loss … that is to say, the body running away from food's nutritive value… the little I could swallow producing no effect ...

The town physician said it might be the liver, or perhaps an accelerated metabolism, or still a rather more complex neural problem: the brain can get all mixed up and start giving out the wrong orders to the digestive system. Everything good is thrown out, in wee and in pooh, and what is no good, along with every toxin, is thrown back into the blood: it's been known to happen! But please don't worry, we need to take a better look into things, ask for new medical exams, these first tests are not at all conclu-sive. Meanwhile, tell me what you've been eating ever since you got the first symptoms.

Technical queries are useful but, at times, they can turn into sheer banality because science, when it takes a wrong turn, it's just like the economy or the arts:

it looses its bearings and becomes a helpless child, lost in a strange city.

I summed-up my last major supper and the doctor opened his mouth, in anguish

"Hell! Now I'm starving!"

and

"Be that as it may, I really don't think that has … but thirteen hours of nonstop eating? You gobblers!"

The lunch-plus-dinner-in-one was a masterpiece created by a food artist, Chef Vintém. This talented young man's goal—and, by the bye, he weights the same as two men, without being fat—is a noble and revolutionary one: to reinstate in people's consumption habits, gaining entrance through international haute cuisine's grandiose gate, the roughest, ugliest, greasiest, most sinewy, colorless, gristly and inedible, so to speak, parts of an animal.

To build lightness within heaviness, to give delicacy to the stench of mutton, to make poetry from bacon: brief summary as this may be, it encompasses the essential. Master Vintém wants to tear down the conservative notions about healthy food that nowadays, in their zeal to combat the famous "plastic food in hamburgers and pizza", have become too radical. Forgetting that, for example, our ancestors used to say, referring to pigs, that everything, but everything can be put to good use. If nothing else, the Chef says, at least out of respect for the human-swine physiological likeness.

A pig is in everything similar to us, in terms of internal anatomy. Anyone who has seen a pig cut open, and I've seen a few, laying there on the slab, almost smiling in spite of its noisy defeat against the knife, squirting into the basin, with its hair scorched by the burning herbs or by a portable torch: whoever has looked inside a pig was able to see his own viscera in the mirror. Everything, but everything, has the same size. The testicles, well, those are way larger except, because they have already been cut off —pigs are gelded not to compromise the meat's taste— nobody ever notices it.

To compare testicles, one should look at the rooster's, for it has a pair to mach our own, which is obviously why it rules the roost, a most amazing thing, by the way.

Some day, we'll be wearing the kidneys and even the hearts of pigs, medical routes are headed that way, all they need is to find the substance, I don't know what exactly, that makes the transfusion viable and we'll have our lives extended. I'm not so sure this will be available in time for me, and I certainly wouldn't mind prolonging my travels for another hundred years, but I really don't believe it. Organ grafting between different animal species: I bet there's already a bunch of stuff about this subject in the Internet. On second thoughts, if it means having a pig's heart in my chest, I'd sooner die right away.

Vintém started the meal with bacon carpaccio—transparent lamellas of lard, in the raw—asparagus omelet made from duck eggs, breaded pork brains—deep-fried in olive oil—but please notice:

"Inside, the brain is almost raw ..."

"The soft texture of a sponge!"

"Its color! Its aroma!"

Next, we had cows' foot sinews and pigs' feet, each in a double presentation of coriander and tomato sauces. Again, these were—incredibly—fried, in a thin fritter batter of powdery breadcrumbs, allowing for the moist and the flavor to remain intact on the inside. After this, came the thymus in garlic and the mutton testicles, chopped in little pieces, in a whitish sauce, which is made of, huh, tells us, Chef Vintém, what's in this sauce?

"What d'ya think? See what happens if you cook yours."

A huge head, roasted in the oven with aromatic herbs, and yet, prepared in a way not distant from the impossible because the head presented itself deboned in the tray, thoroughly removed from the skull without loosing its shape, it was a black pork's mask, a rounded scalp of the snout and the ears, it was like eating a very ugly man's face.

After a while and after the wine, fresh scallops were announced, causing a commotion, us being so far from the coast and all.

"These scallops come from the cork oak forest."

"Scallops from the cork oak forest?"

"Scallops that grow in the countryside."

and it was true: over crackers, the round interior—immaculate—of a bivalve, rosy and steam cooked, that turned out to be a cow's spinal cord cut into slices! A several hundred pound animal that grazes in the fields transformed into seafood! Artists can deceive our senses and make us see things that are very different things after all. Hidden parts of the world. And by doing so, they make us think, I don't know if you would agree.

"Today, my friends, we're like the ancient Romans."

"One day, civilization ended and barbarity followed. We must restore civilization."

I believe it was around midnight, with the bathroom already filthy—someone didn't stomach the banquet—that we had the hedgehog stew, served with tiny potatoes and leek. The Chef assured us it wasn't a menstruated female and that, therefore, it wasn't poisonous. It occurred to someone that hedgehog skin is great to make gloves from, the kind you stuff teenagers' hands into who devote themselves to onanism on the Internet, instead of studying. Then, I told the mole story ...

"I never tasted mole. Badger treats, yes, and raven and stork ..."

"Shush!"

and of how we killed and buried them under the chestnut tree, in a common grave. Everyone at the table was silent and sadness filled the night because it had been a very nasty thing, killing so many nice little creatures using broken glass. Broken glass! How they must have suffered ... Sometimes, I hang around that place and I think of them. But we had no choice, the moles ate the olive trees' roots, it takes a man to do a man's job.

Chef Vintém sat down, folded his arms and said that there is a lot of suffering going on in every corner of the world, in some places more than others, sure, but misfortune can come knocking at our door, anytime. Here we are, our bellies full, maybe even too full, shame on me, but every single day twenty five thousand people die from lack of food and this should make us wonder about one thing: the effects of starvation in man and, consequently, on what we call civilization. What I mean is, Vintém said, in the 20th century, sometime after the great holocausts and genocides but before the most recent ones, a disturbing discovery was made in Africa, in northeastern Uganda. There were a people who used to call themselves the Mountain People, but whom everyone else called the Iks, a name like a hiccup. Their "finder", British anthropologist Colin Turnbull, who lived among them for many months, came to the conclusion that they were, probably, the "worst people in the world". For starters, when one of the Iks broke into laughter, rolling on the floor, it might very well be because he had spent three consecutive days without eating a thing. In their language, the term for a "good man" was simply a "full belly man". Familial bonds, a disgrace: the stronger Iks kept all the food they could find to themselves. It was normal for a mother to laugh if she dropped her baby on the floor, hurting the child. This bizarre wretchedness, so it seems, was due to the prohibition—a few years earlier, when the Government created an ecological wildlife reserve—which forbade them from hunting in their ancestral territories, as their forefathers had always done. The Iks decided to stay but the soil was poor and not even goats could feed from it. The Iks economy became a spiritual tragedy. Surviving by cruelty, Turnbull wrote. But none of this can explain what came next. One day, a woman was distracted—or did it on purpose—and lost her baby when she was looking for water away from the village. Everyone assumed a leopard had caught the baby. And this, the anthropologist established, filled the Iks with hope: in the next few hours, or days, a sleepy and satisfied leopard would most likely appear in that area, in the shade of a shrub. And that is exactly what happened: they found the leopard, the one that swallowed the little boy—but for a piece of the skull—they killed it, boiled it and ate all of it, "including the child."

The cook unfolded his arms and asked me:

"If you were starving to death, wouldn't you eat the leopard?"

I can't get rid of this idea.

Translated from the Portuguese by Maria João Medeiros.
The original title of this short story is Estômago Animal.

As you would have told it to me (sort of) if we had known each other before you died

Jonas Hassen Khemiri

I remember that it was fall. And that it was a weekend. And that I was sitting at home drinking apple juice and half-watching a rerun of a debate program. My neighbor across the courtyard had bought a new TV and he was watching the same channel. It felt nice, somehow. That we were sitting on our respective sides of the courtyard and. I don't know. Sharing something. I hadn't spoken with K in three days. But I wasn't worried. It was like that between us sometimes. Soon she would call and we'd meet up and everything would be. Like normal. It didn't mean that we were on the way to breaking up. We had gotten through worse things. I wasn't worried.

It was probably around lunchtime when the doorbell rang. I turned off the TV. Across the courtyard I could see that the debate program was still on. The local politician's brow was furrowed. The average mom shook her head. The host lobbed a question to the audience. The doorbell rang again. Once. Twice. I sat perfectly still and dead silent because I knew. Or I thought. That it was my annoying neighbor. The one who lived under me and had gotten it into his head that I had visitors late at night. He had rung at my door a few times. Always pissed off. Always with the same demand: that I really must tell my guests to talk with "lowercase letters" after midnight. That's what he said. Every time. And when I explained that I hadn't even had any guests over and that the yelling must have come from a different apartment, he looked kind of. Skeptical. And a little afraid.

But. There was something about this ringing that felt. I don't know. Different. Suddenly I got it into my head that it was K ringing my bell. Maybe she wanted to say she was sorry. Cross out what had happened. I sneaked toward the hall and looked out through the peephole. Police. The whole stairwell was full of police. Dark blue jackets. Stern expressions. Nearest the door stood a blond policewoman with a packet of snus under her lip. In the back, a red-headed policeman who had taken out his baton. In reality, there were probably only four or five of them, but there was something about the peephole perspective that turned them into an army. I was terrified. I stood there on the hall rug with palpitations and a dry tongue. Not because I had done anything, but because. I don't know why. Maybe because there were so many of them. And they looked so angry. I made a snap decision. I decided not to open the door. Under no circumstances would I unlock it or make my presence known. I would sneak back to the living room, take a gulp of apple juice, and sit in complete silence until they disappeared. That was my strategy. And it might have worked. If the one in front hadn't suddenly opened the mail slot and looked in. I felt the rush of air from the stairwell against my bare knees, and I heard a voice that said: Nice cutoffs. And. I don't know but. I was so surprised that I stretched out my hand and unlocked the door.

The police stormed in, the hall was filled with uniforms, someone secured the rest of the apartment while the one with the snus dealt with me. She told me to put my hands on my head and spread my legs. But but but, I said. There must be some mistake. I'm a civil engineer. Oh, how nice for you, she said. No, I mean. I. I studied at the Royal Institute of Technology. I just got a permanent position at the Patent and Registration Office. I'm from Motala!

Is that so, she said and nodded to her red-headed colleague, who stood ready with the handcuffs.

On the way down in the elevator I stopped resisting. My body realized that it was pointless. But my mouth continued to say a lot of things that my brain barely understood. I said that I hadn't defaulted on any debt payments. That I never hopped the turnstiles on the subway. That I worked out at Friskis & Svettis. When we came out of the front door I pointed at a car that was parked a little down the street and I heard myself say something completely bizarre: Do you see that gray Volvo over there? It's mine. I don't know why I said it. My Volvo was white. And was parked two blocks away.

The policeman led me along to the police car. My body was sweaty and cold and my mouth babbled on while the policeman was completely silent and seemed to be thinking of other things. My mouth said that my apartment was two-and-a-half-rooms and fifty-five square meters and the balcony almost but only almost faced south. My mouth said that I was completely one hundred percent innocent. My mouth said that I was getting married this summer.

And it was only at this point that I started to suspect something. The policeman, who until now had had an indifferent, stony face, suddenly got a little smile on his lips. It kind of fluttered up across his face. If you can say that. And at first I thought I was seeing things. But when I said that I had been engaged to K for two years and that the wedding was finally going to happen, on Öland next summer, it looked like the policeman was trying to keep from laughing. And then. Finally. I understood what was going on.

The "policeman" led me to the police car and locked me in the backseat. I did my best to play the innocent accused. I shook my head dejectedly. I sighed and mumbled: This is completely scandalous. I didn't say thanks when he unlocked my handcuffs. But it wasn't easy. Because honestly. Aren't you happy when you realize that your friends remember you. Isn't it great when you're reminded that you're actually not alone, that you have friends out there who care about you. Even if you haven't spoken in a few years. Even if you live in different cities and maybe have lost touch a little.

I imagined that they would start it off with a classic champagne breakfast. The police car starts the sirens and drives me at lightning speed to a park where the whole gang has gathered—Anders L, Omid, Nico, and Egg. And then Miro, of course. Miro who has planned everything. Miro who sees me get out of the police car and we look at each other and he smiles and I say: You fucker, you god-damn fucking nut! But I say it in that joking way that friends have when they're saying mean things about each other that both realize are a joke. Miro flies at me and we fall all over the grass and get stains on our knees and alternately hug and fight until we're exhausted. Then he leads me over to the others, who have laid out one of those thick, plaid blankets that families have when they have picnics at Djurgården. An abundance of alcohol, bakery bread, sausages with complicated names, cheeses you cut with a knife. There's a toast and we drain our glasses and throw them over our shoulders so they break, because we have tons of glasses and you only get married once. Or three times, says Egg, and we understand that he's referring to himself and everyone laughs the way true friends do when they know each other well enough.

It took longer than expected. The "policeman" who was guarding me took out his phone and wrote a text. Presumably he was texting Miro that everything had gone according to plan. I could tell that I was smiling again and I tried to force my lips down into a terse, expressionless face.

Then we go out on the town and first we do that thing I heard a colleague saying on the phone that her sister had had to do for her bachelorette party. My friends take out a video camera and put me in a swimming ring, diving flippers, a bikini, and a diving mask, and then I have to walk around the city and sell hugs. Everyone who sees us gets that I have a bunch of friends who've planned this for me and no one thinks that they're doing it to be mean. Even though I think it's going to be annoying and embarrassing, it ends with big laughs and lots of hugs. Then we move on to a recording studio where I have to do the same thing that my dentist told me that his son got for a bachelor party present—record a song to his future wife, and at first of course I say: No, I can't sing, I have a terrible voice. But the whole gang and most of all Miro are just: No, come on, you can, you can, and when I start singing the studio tech is a little shocked and says: Wow, what pipes. Everyone in the gang cheers and sings along in the refrain and the studio tech asks if it's okay if he saves the recording and maybe gets in touch sometime if he needs someone to lay down some vocals. Then there's some archery and a sauna and a seven-course dinner at a fancy restaurant. Or else we go out in the woods and play paintball or go bowling or play floorball at the borrowed office of an architect with a view out over the whole city. Miro laughs the whole time and says: You looked scared as shit when you got out of the police car, and I play along and say: Yeah, you're right. You totally got me. Everything felt one hundred percent real.

And it really did. It was the little details that were most impressive. Like that the police car didn't smell like a rental car and instead had dirty windows and dusty floormats and smelled like prawn salad from a half-eaten baguette that someone had left in the front seat. And that the driver finally came down and had something on her nail that she scraped off on a light pole. And that the guy who'd been waiting sat right down on the baguette so it stuck to the back of his uniform pants and the lower part of his police shirt. And that the driver laughed and the passenger swore and the driver helped him get the worst of the goo off with a wet wipe that smelled like airplane.

I sat there in the back seat and thought that either they were real police who did this on the side. Or else they were really crazy good actors. When we had been driving for a few minutes I leaned toward the black net that separated the front and back seats and whispered: You two are totally incredible. Excuse me? Said the guy playing the passenger policeman. Oh, nothing, I said. Then I leaned back and tried to keep in the laughter that bubbled in my stomach. I felt happier than I had for. I don't know how long. The police looked at each other and the driver met my eyes in the rearview mirror. No one said anything but there was an unspoken feeling of solidarity between us. We had some sort of unity. Some sort of. I don't know what. When the traffic increased the driver finally turned on the siren and cars veered off sideways and gave us the right of way. The sound from the sirens seemed muffled somehow. As though it were another police car several blocks away and not ours. It still smelled like airplane mixed with prawn salad.

If it had been a normal bachelor party organized by a normal gang of friends, we would have gone directly to the champagne breakfast. But Miro and the gang were more ambitious than that. Miro wanted me to have a bachelor party that would go down in history. I understood that when the police car drove up to the jail. Or. The place that was supposed to represent the jail. And which must have been somewhere on Kungsholmen—not far from the real jail. At first I suspected that we were in a school that was closed for the weekend, because the forms and the binders in the office where I was booked in reminded me of a teacher's lounge, and the extras who were playing criminals waiting for family looked suspiciously young. But then when we started to walk through the wide corridors with markings painted on the floor and buzzing strip lights on the ceiling, I started to suspect that Miro and the gang had rented a hospital. No matter where we were, it was impressive. Particularly the interrogation room, because it really looked exactly like an interrogation room. A lone light hanging from the ceiling, a fake mirror on the wall, a table, and two chairs. And the guy who was playing the interrogator, of course. A typical grumpy bad cop who smiled scornfully when I said that I didn't need a lawyer because I was totally one hundred percent *innocent*. I don't know why I said it in English. But it sounded good. The policeman asked a lot of questions about me and K, how we met, when we last saw each other, what I had been doing on Thursday night between 10 pm and midnight. I mostly sat silently and looked down at the table and tried not let the fact that his mustache was crooked irritate me. Once he said something that I thought was really quite mean and then I was close to leaning forward and ripping off his fake mustache. But I controlled myself. I listened to his questions and only answered when there was a chance to say something nice about K. Because I knew, of course, that Miro and the gang were standing and snickering behind that fake mirror and sometimes I looked in toward the room on the other side and smiled at the camera because I assumed that they were filming everything in order to edit it all together for one of those charming films that they would show at the wedding. I looked into the mirror and explained to myself and the camera and the future wedding guests that I have never loved anyone the way I love K. She is the most beautiful person in the world. Both inside and out. In some magical way she makes me into a better version of myself. She's perfect. One hundred percent perfect. I wouldn't change a thing about her. Not her morning mood. Not how she gets when she's been drinking. Not her underbite. The questioning policeman hmmed and pretended to jot something in the notebook he had in front of him.

Near the end of the interrogation, he asked again what I thought of the accusations, and then I said I had forgotten them. He repeated the accusations. I said that I had forgotten them again. The whole time I was thinking up a good conclusion. He repeated them again in an angry voice and I answered: I want a lawyer—even if this process is just one big joke! I saw before me how Miro and the gang were laughing themselves to pieces on the other side of the mirror.

After the interrogation I was taken to my "cell." It wasn't as impressive as the interrogation room. Not to sound ungrateful, but here it was obvious that Miro and the gang had. How should I put it. Been a little stingy. Instead of fixing up a real cell with a dirty floor, free-standing toilet, and the kind of bars that the guards drag their batons along, they shut me in a small yellow-painted room with shelves on the wall, a desk of light wood, and a fat TV without a remote. Instead of having to sleep in a rickety bunk bed above a tattooed, snoring fellow prisoner with a razor blade behind his upper lip, I got a completely normal bed with sheets, a mattress, and a wall-mounted reading lamp. Instead of risking being raped in the shower by a gang of threatening bikers with walrus mustaches, I was presented to the day guard Thomas who welcomed me to my room in a soft voice and recommended that I get some rest before fish sticks and mashed potatoes were served for dinner. Is there juice? I asked. Thomas nodded. Everything felt more or less like a hostel. Only the door was metal, had a peephole that you couldn't see out of, and was locked 24 hours a day.

The first night was a little rough. But I reminded

myself that I wasn't alone. I lay on my mattress, which smelled summery from detergent. I listened to the silence. I looked up at the ceiling and imagined how my friends were sitting in an exactly identical room on the other side of the wall with surveillance headphones on and a big whirring tape reel in the background. They tried to keep from laughing when they saw me looking around for hidden cameras. After a while I started to wave at them and speak to them. I looked toward the ventilation duct and said: Hi, Miro, hi, Egg. Shit, what a circus you've started. You're crazy to do all of this for me. But that's enough now, okay? Come out now. When I didn't get an answer I lay quietly and imagined how I looked on the black and white surveillance screen. My grainy body, like an almost transparent phantom. I looked credible as I was lying there on the bed. It didn't look like I was crying.

My "lawyer" was played by a professional woman with black hair and a briefcase that must have been bought second-hand, because it looked believably worn out. When I asked her if she also knew Miro and the gang she looked at me so intensely that I felt like a mirror in an interrogation room. For the last time, she said. I don't know "Miro" or his so-called "gang." If you want to try playing confused in the courtroom you may. But you don't need to do it with me. I know that you know that I am a real lawyer. I know that you know that this is a real jail. And I hope that you understand that you have been accused of a real crime that will be tried in the Stockholm District Court. They have found your sooty sweatjacket, they have witnesses who saw you on her balcony. You're risking a lengthy prison sentence. Do you understand? I nodded and thought: She's good. She is really damn good. Did her homework. Convincing. At first I thought she was a little miscast because she chewed gum and had a kind of tic where she touched behind her ear with her finger and then smelled the finger. But now. After her outburst. I realized that she was perfect. Before she left she leaned toward me and said: Hey. Think about whether you really want to continue this act. Because I don't think it's going to help you. Between us, you're not particularly convincing. But you are, I thought. But didn't say anything. She got up and put her papers in her briefcase, which was so wrong that in some way it became right. And so old that it left behind little black flakes of leather on the table.

I don't remember much of the trial itself. I had slept badly. The days had started to run together. I felt feverish and weak. The judge spoke and my lawyer spoke and the prosecutor spoke and sometimes I raised my gaze from the table and saw how fake everything looked. Miro and the gang must have run out of money, because this room was so inauthentic that no one could take it seriously. It looked like a large classroom. The wood was light instead of dark. The judge had on a baggy gray suit instead of one of those dress-like things with a white wig. The jurors' box, which should have been enclosed by a little railing, was replaced by a regular table, and instead of a jury there were three half-asleep retirees playing lay judges. The prosecutor read the paper during breaks and didn't yell: Objection, Your Honor, a single time. Not even the onlookers' benches felt authentic, because they were completely empty except for K's sisters with their clumsily made-up eyes. Once in the middle of it all, a school class came in; they sat down and listened for a few minutes; the students yawned; the teacher looked at a bus timetable. Then they got up and left. I remained seated next to my lawyer and thought that they were probably just as disappointed as I was. No one disrupted the order, no one came rushing in screaming: This man is innocent, no one cried besides K's sisters. But they were fake tears. The actors playing the witnesses claimed to have seen me outside K's apartment. A young man with a full beard said that I'd climbed up on the dumpster next to the streetlight outside her bedroom. A lady said that she'd been out walking her dog and saw me jump down from the balcony and almost get caught in the rosebushes. A few minutes later she'd seen the first flames. It was so obvious the witnesses were lying that I couldn't even pretend to be upset. I just sat there and felt sick and feverish. Then it was K's turn to take the stand but she didn't want to do it while I was in the room. I understood. She probably wouldn't be able to keep from laughing if she saw me. Just as I was being escorted out she came in from another direction and our eyes met for one maybe two seconds and at first I wasn't sure it was really her because they'd made up her cheeks with bubbling yellowish blisters and on her throat I could see black marks and one arm was wrapped in a bandage. I wanted to smile at her and say: Soon it will all be over. But I didn't have time because the guard closed the door.

The verdict came sooner than expected and apparently that was a bad sign, my lawyer said, but I didn't care. I just wanted it all to be over. I just wanted the cell door to be opened and Miro and the gang would come rushing in and shout: SURPRISE! Suddenly I would have a bouquet in one hand and a glass of champagne in the other and all the actors and extras and cameramen would come out from behind the scenes and stand in a big circle and applaud when Miro gave a toast for the world's best friend. But instead I was led back into the courtroom that didn't look like a courtroom. The judge who didn't look like a judge read the verdict, which didn't sound like a verdict. Afterward everyone looked at me. As though they were waiting for me to. I don't know. Say something. But I was quiet. I had nothing to add. The judge banged his little gavel on the table and no one applauded and no one booed, no journalists wanted to ask questions and I didn't need to put a jacket over my head when I was led out of the room, because there were no photographers who wanted to take my picture.

I was led back to my yellow-painted cell. K went home to her smoke-smelling stairwell. I was moved to an institution. She moved to a new apartment with a secret address. I spent my days packing black and sometimes brown shoelaces in transparent plastic packaging. She spent her days putting ointment on her blisters and calling the insurance company. I spent my nights dreaming of Miro and the gang. She spent her nights dreaming of me.

I was released after three years. Or a little more than three years. Almost four. I went right home to my old apartment. I put on my cutoffs, sat on the sofa with a glass of apple juice, and turned on the TV. It was a documentary about hyenas and I looked out at the courtyard to see if my neighbor might be watching the same show. But he had moved. Or else he had put the TV in a different room. It made me. Not sad but. I don't know. For several weeks I tried to get into playing the role of myself. Sometimes I thought about contacting K. Sometimes I walked past her old apartment. Once I called up her work and said I was a friend who wanted to plan a surprise party for her and so I would need her new address. They said that unfortunately they couldn't give it out. The second time I called I got disconnected. The third time I don't remember what happened.

Eight months later I died in a moped accident in Portugal. One week later I was resurrected in Stockholm when K found out what had happened. Suddenly I was back in her life. I lay beside her when she woke. I followed her when she ran to the bus. I gave her a thumbs up if she made a sale and I comforted her when she collapsed in the bathroom at work with the faucet running so no one would hear her crying. At night I watched over her. I stood on her balcony and looked into her bedroom with the palms of my hands like two white parentheses pressed against the glass. Soon she got used to it. Soon she stopped waking with a start when she saw my silhouette. It was almost like we. Were together again. Like we gave each other one last chance. In the evenings I followed her to dinner with her girlfriends and I didn't sigh when she wanted to take a taxi and I didn't say that she had too much makeup on in the elevator on the way up. I didn't clear my throat when she poured her third glass of wine before the appetizer. I didn't imitate her when she began to slur her words. I wasn't ashamed when she suddenly rolled up her sleeve and showed everyone the pitted, reddened burn on her arm. Hey, look at this, she shouted. You all can complain as much as you want about your partners who forget to buy milk or who clip their toenails at the kitchen table, because my former relationship was a real trial by fire! Her friends laughed. Maybe I needed to light a fire under myself to understand that I should end it! Her friends' laughter was a little more forced. Or else it was my fault because I was playing with fire, or no, I had too many irons in the fire! And at this point her friends stopped laughing and asked the hostess if she needed help in the kitchen. When K went to the bathroom to throw up, I held her damp forehead, and when she had wiped her mouth with the back of her hand and wanted to go home, I helped her put on her shoes. The fake me lay in a morgue in Portugal, waiting to be trans-ported home. The real me wandered toward home with K on a warm summer night. She held my hand unnecessarily hard and whispered: Don't leave me don't leave me don't leave me.

The next day, K told her older sister what had happened. I. The only person who had really loved her. Was dead. K's older sister sighed and did her best to comfort her. Then she hung up and told her partner that I. That crazy sadist who had stalked her little sister. Was dead. Her sister's partner told her lover, the lover told her orthopedist, the orthopedist told his squash partner. The squash partner told his colleague who told her babysitter who told you. My name roamed on. From mouth to mouth. From living room to hotel room, from waiting room to dressing room, from conference room to bedroom. Haven't you heard? I'm dead. I rented a moped in Portugal. I crashed into a billboard. A taxi opened its door and I didn't have a helmet on. I drove off a cliff. I drove into a river. I had just been set free. I had been out for six months. I had been found guilty of attempted murder. I was put away for manslaughter. I was convicted for arson. She died. She survived. She suffered burns. She was in a coma. She was fine. Poor her. Serves her right. She had tried to break up. She had just met someone. She had been cheating for eight months with a guy at her work called Filip Widell. It was all in my imagination. I climbed up on a dumpster and saw it with my own eyes. I threw a firebomb through the kitchen window. I poured gasoline through the mail slot. I accidentally set fire to a mattress on her balcony. I was drunk. I was sober. I was high. I was psychotic. I wanted to a make an anti-capitalist statement. I wanted to collect insurance money. I was alone. I was tragic. I was jealous. I was in love. I was studying at the Royal Institute of Technology. I had graduated from the Royal Institute of Technology. I was a civil engineer. I was in your grade at school. I was arrested and thought that it was all just a bachelor party.

When you hear my name you recognize it, but you have to go home and get out an old yearbook to remember my face. There I am. Third from the left in the middle row. With a white polo collar sticking up under the v-necked sweater. I'm standing obediently turned, with my shoulder toward the photographer. I'm smiling. I could be anyone at all. You have. No memory of me. Or. Wait. You remember that we played floorball together a few times in the schoolyard. That I spoke a dialect. And that I had cutoffs with super cool frayed edges. Once you were standing behind me in the line for the juice machines in the lunchroom and when I turned around I had two glasses of apple juice instead of one and. Somehow you were impressed that I had realized that you could take two glasses at once. That's all you remember of me. And still you decide to try to change yourself into me. Based on rumors and fragmented memories and two newspaper articles and a verdict from the Stockholm District Court, you write a text in my voice. You put me in cutoffs. You force extreme amounts of apple juice into me. You let me believe that everything, absolutely everything, is one big bachelor party.

You have a great time trespassing in my life, and it's not until the end. About. Here. That you realize you've failed. Again. Because deep down, you know very well who's sitting up at night and talking to himself so loudly that the neighbor on the floor below has started to complain. Deep down, you know who has a friend named Miro who died three years ago and who is never coming back. I'm not the one fantasizing about fancy picnics at Djurgården or imagining I have a good singing voice. I'm not the one making up imaginary friends and smuggling puns into their names. I have no problem living in reality. I can trust people. You're the one dreaming that one day the cell door will be opened and Miro will be standing there with his smile saying: You're free now.

Translated from the Swedish by Rachel Willson-Broyles. The original title of this short story is Så som du hade berättat det för mig (ungefär) om vi hade lärt känna varandra innan du dog.

The Cancellation

Emmanuelle Pagano

I recognized you instantly, from the back, by your walk, by the way you have of walking that leaves you slightly off-balance, strained. Not exactly a limp, not injured, no, just a little bent, a little askew. I stopped. You turned, and I saw your nametag even before I saw your face. No doubt about it, it was you. Your face, you folded it inward as if you were trying to hide it. You got into the car without resistance, but then, what was there to resist. You were hitchhiking, I stopped, and it seemed to you that it was all happening at once, you didn't recognize me, what was there to resist. You didn't look at me, you tried to hide your wrinkled and troubled and trembling face, how could you have recognized me.

You got in, you buckled your seat belt, and, very slowly, as if it was painful, you unfolded, you brought your face out of your body, and you looked at me. You stared at me, and I could see in your eyes that my face meant something to you, but what. You couldn't place me, you recognized me without recognizing me. You had seen my face somewhere, and here it was, in front of you, in front of you and somewhere else, too, in a reluctant memory, my known-but-not-recognized face, my face like a word on the tip of your tongue. You smiled to say thank you.

It's you, it's you first of all, and it's you above all that we didn't recognize. Not here, in the dusk, hitchhiking by the side of the road, but earlier, all afternoon at the wedding. Even I, I didn't recognize you. How could I have recognized you, you don't look a thing like me, we who used to look so much alike. But no, not you, it was my cousin, my cousin who looked so much like me. My cousin is a little younger than I, and a bit smaller, too.

I remember a game we played as children, a game only we knew, a game entirely ours, hers and mine, my cousin and me. We positioned our faces in facing mirrors, mirrors in the bathroom folded open to just the right angle to show nothing but our profiles. My cousin's face was just below mine, like a repetition, not really a reflection, more like a visible stutter. Her face, the same, my face right below itself, younger, repeated, doubled. We called the game "the drunken mirrors."

There was no way I could have recognized you, as, obviously, you weren't her. Despite your nametag declaring your name, my cousin's name, no one got it, not even me. We got that you weren't her, but we didn't get what you were doing there, nor who you were. We didn't even try to get it. My cousin wasn't there, no doubt held up in traffic, and you, you were there, wearing her name on a nametag. My cousin sometimes forgets her manners; if you're going to be late, you let someone know, and if you're not going to come, you cancel. There are always cancellations at a wedding, even at the last minute. It's a terrible bother, but after all, at the very worst, you simply redo the seating, you shift people, you shuffle them in relation to the head of the table, you reorganize, balancing the number of women and men. It's really rude not to cancel, just as it is not to let people know when you're going to be late, and we had just begun to wonder if my cousin had had an accident when you started calling attention to yourself. At first it took our minds off of worrying about her, but then it began to cause an even greater concern. We all thought, conditioned as we are by our expectations, that it was simply a joke in bad taste, then that you were a glomm-on, as my grandchildren would say. If not, why the name tag? This street person had appropriated our name in order to eat and drink and have a good time on our dime. Above all, to drink, we whispered, your bloated face was clearly that of an alcoholic. You had written our last name on your nametag, my last name, as well as the bride-to-be's, my cousin's too, and you had chosen a first name at random, and had just happened to pick my cousin's, it's a common name. So, all explained. And yet, and now that I know, it's easy, it's easy to understand, and now I remember, I noticed it in passing, but then just as quickly forgot, you didn't drink a single drop of alcohol, and now I know why.

It was the first thing I asked you, once you'd gotten into the car, just after your thank you and your glance, and even before I knew where you were going. Why the nametag. You replied in such a long exhalation that I thought you were going to run out of breath, or were hoping you'd never have to breathe again, would never have to stop speaking, you replied in a single gust of words, and with a mouth so trembling that I had a hard time hearing you, understanding you, you told me and trembled and exhaled your entire history of a woman sick and dependent on constant care.

You have to go back to the diabetic center, now, a nurse is waiting for you to give you your dialysis tomorrow morning, you are lost. You don't know what to do now, your train had been organized by the center, but you had to leave much earlier because, in fact, no, you weren't invited to the wedding, and so you don't know what to do now, how to take a bus back to the train station, all this time to wait, and the bus, and the train. And you couldn't take an earlier train, the ticket was not exchangeable, and you just didn't know, you don't know about things like that, you go out so rarely, almost never. In reality, no, you hadn't thought about it, you had just walked out, no, in anger, you don't really know anymore, it was just then, it was now, and it wasn't all that great an idea because, thanks to leaving earlier you were going to be late, you were maybe even going to miss your train, the evening train, the one you'd initially planned to take, and you were going to miss your dialysis, and if I could oh yes if I could drive you to the station and lend you the price of a ticket to take the earlier train, at least to not miss the evening train, or to help you change your ticket, that would put your mind at ease. All I had to do was to give you my address and the center would pay me back, they're so nice, if I only knew, without them …

You weren't looking at me anymore, again. You mixed up the timetables, the times, you were completely disoriented. Again you had pulled your face back into your body. I promised all of the above, yes of course, naturally. And then, and only then, you breathed again, and you turned your face toward me. A face that anyone, anyone and first of all I, would have recognized clearly as that of an alcoholic, a face marked, tracked, inevitably by drink, the skin swollen, crossed by tiny exploded capillaries, fatty and blemished, embryonic evidence of I don't know what infection, those light eyes washed out and red, those prematurely old eyes looked at me. You looked at me for such a long time that I was afraid you'd recognize me, but this was an absent look, and in its vacancy, tears swelled. You cried voluptuously now, you cried with as much energy as you had put to explaining yourself a moment before, but without words, and from then on, without anger. Your face finally understandable, justified by the tears, all that redness and puffiness excused, explained by the tears. You smiled at me and I understood that you had still not recognized me, perhaps thanks to the tears. You thanked me and made good use of the Kleenex that I'd just given you, I don't really know if you thanked me, but something close to it, with a loud blowing of the nose and an inelegant mouth. Nothing about you is elegant, that's the least that can be said, and perhaps that's what so upset my daughter. Mother, look how she's dressed, she said, and I said to her but look at yourself, dear, look what a state you're in, it's not that big a deal, pull yourself together. You caught your breath, again, yes, took a deep breath and this time without trembling you told me how kind I was, like the people at the center, and not like the bride.

When you said that word, I started, realizing that, in my haste, I hadn't taken all the decorations off the car, and, as if I'd spoken my thoughts out loud, as if you had translated my sudden start, had fully understood, you smiled very discretely, almost to yourself, asking me if I too was going to, or had just come from, a wedding. You added, embarrassed, that I was so well dressed, while you, well, you simply didn't have the means. I replied that I was coming from my daughter's wedding. Nothing less. You seemed reassured, saying that of course, if I was Family (you didn't say "one of the family" but "Family," leaning on the capital, and you, who could you be if you weren't Family), you seemed reassured as if such a close relationship with the bride justified such grand style much more than social convention, means, rank, or indecent buying power ever could have. Besides, those people, those at the wedding you went to, the wedding you're coming back from, or rather not coming back from, you never come back from such a thing, because of their lack of tact, those people, no matter how well dressed they were, like me (you said "like you" with a knowing air as if you had finally recognized me, but upon reflection, that's impossible), those people so well dressed, they didn't have a very becoming attitude. You pronounced the word "becoming" as if you held it with tongs, afraid of its contaminating filth. It's really a shame to dress with so much taste, and then to follow it up with so little elegance. You had an invitation, you could show it to me if I didn't believe you, you had an invitation for the wedding. You were angry again. I believed you.

I couldn't believe it.

That invitation, I had written the address down on the calligrapher's list myself, I'd spent more time on it than on any of the others, I had to dig it out, it took several hours on the Internet, and finally I'd found a kind of post-office box. My cousin was always what we called eccentric, I wasn't surprised by your address, I never even thought it might be somebody else's, our name isn't that common. This name, we think of it as prestigious, rare. A name of rank.

You came back to yourself. You looked at me for a long time, excusing yourself for taking me out of my way, you were perhaps going to make me miss my daughter's wedding, that would be inconceivable, or it would be unconscionable, I couldn't quite hear you, but suddenly you realized, and you wanted me to stop right there and leave you by the side of the road. By the side of the highway. "Out of the question," I hissed, which also meant, "Drop the question" to cut the conversation short. It wasn't what I wanted, on the contrary, I wanted to hear everything that you had to say to me, I wanted to interrogate you again and again, but I didn't want to say too much about my presence here, on this highway, in my best wedding clothes. I wanted to know more, much more, I wanted to ask questions, all the questions, but I didn't want to answer yours.

What I want to know most of all is who are you? Who are you, tell me, if you're not my cousin?

I will still have doubts, you know, looking at the photos of the wedding a few days later. It was just when they were taking photos on the steps of the church that your behavior had started seeming odd. You wanted to be photographed with the newlyweds, and of course they refused. You thought it was a joke, then you tried to sneak into the picture from the side. And I think you actually managed to get into a few. I will look at them and I will wonder if it was you, or my cousin, if she had changed, if you are my cousin, if you no longer look like me. If she had fallen ill. No, she would have told me, she would have been surprised, she would have laughed: but don't you even recognize me? She would have laughed instead of declaring, as you did, that you had been invited, that no one could kick you out like that. Instead of protesting and yet not being able to prove any connection with the wedding couple. Because that's the question we asked in order to have the intruder removed, we asked you if you were related to one of the people getting married. Or it really was you, my cousin, but you had lost your head, your memory. She had lost her memory and had looked at us without understanding, incapable of answering the question except by showing your invitation, my invitation, the invitation whose address it had taken me so much time to find, the invitation that I had sent, now thrust out feverishly, like a pass. And we, we dismissed you, we handed the invitation back, there must be some error, Ma'am, you understand.

But you didn't understand, no, you made a scene, that's what my daughter said, she didn't want this bag lady crashing her wedding, this nutcase making a scene, and I, I was so ashamed, I held back, yes, I didn't do a thing either way, I just watched from a distance, I was ashamed of my daughter's behavior, of yours, I was ashamed of our error, my error, because I was beginning to understand, I was standing too far back to read the address on the invitation's envelope, but I understood, yes, I suddenly understood, I kept well off to the side, which is why you didn't recognize me when you got into the car.

My one move, my one impulse, my one decision was radical, and after the fact. I left the wedding. I left the wedding after the appetizers, I left my own daughter's wedding,

I ran out on them. You ran out on us, those were pretty much the exact words she texted me a few minutes ago on my cell phone, followed by a question mark. My daughter is so vulgar when she loses it, she who's usually so proper. Yes, I left, just like that, without telling anyone, just as we were going over to the dinner, walked off the estate where at that very moment the grand dinner for the grand wedding of my daughter was, right now, taking place. I took a wrong turn, I took the other route, the highway, to try to find my cousin who wasn't there, and now here we are, both of us, we're in my car, my non-cousin and me. You and me.

I look at you and I won't get over it, won't get over abandoning my daughter on her wedding day, I abandoned her for you, you whom I don't know, you who are nothing to me, you who are not of the family, you whom I nonetheless met at my daughter's wedding, you who were not invited, you who were only invited through my error, my fault, you whom I invited, it's my error who was invited, you who have been made guilty of an involuntary identity theft, you whom I made guilty of this theft. All the same, I'm furious with you, you could have figured it out, guessed, you didn't know those people, so why would they have invited you to their wedding? Why did you accept the invitation? You should have declined. If you'd thought about it for two minutes, you wouldn't have put yourself in this situation, you wouldn't have put us in this situation. I'm angry with you, but I'm here, I'll take you to the station, make sure that you get back to your center, then I'll go back, regretfully, to the celebration. I'll invent a last-minute cancellation for my cousin to avoid any questions.

The discrete—called "background"—music that played during the appetizers is still running through my head. I'm still enveloped in the hiss of the CD, but is it this music, the background music of my daughter's wedding, or the memory of another music, perhaps a music that belongs to no one but you, a musical murmur that must have come from you because it was you that I was looking at during the appetizers, I was watching you struggle, you had been accused, and I said nothing, I wrapped myself up in the musical background, I rooted myself there, in the contrast between the modest music and your anger, in the gap between discretion itself, this felted music, and your vulgarity in defending yourself, in wanting to stay among us, in wanting to join us at the dinner. This music in my head is your obstinacy. Now you beat its rhythm with your fingers on your thigh, I think you're beating out the rhythm of an unknown music, unknown like you, a music that belongs only to you, an interior musical murmur, and this murmur, this music, you only let it out through the tips of your fingers.

During the appetizers you asked so many questions, like a fearless child consumed by curiosity, in a desire to know that went beyond bounds, you went beyond our bounds, the bounds of our implicit social codes, those of appropriate behavior, beyond even the bounds of the background music, so carefully chosen by my daughter, that soft music in which we sheltered. You broke the ambiance, with your questions, you broke the rhythm. I think it was in this rhythmic disorder that you truly seemed like an intruder. You drooled a little, too. You couldn't manage to hold your tongue, you asked so many questions, and you couldn't even manage to keep it in your mouth, that tongue, when you had finished speaking. It came out in an uncontrolled motion, it licked the corners of your lips, and quickly went back in. There was still a little saliva at the edge of your mouth. It was embarrassing, so embarrassing if you had known. But you did know, you knew it perfectly well. You must have noticed the sudden void all around you, the uneasy glances, you must have realized how improper you were being.

They were so disturbing, all your questions punctuated by your clicking tongue, that one of the caterers tried to make you stop. It was effort wasted, you continued to open your mouth, forgetting yourself completely. You asked questions with your mouth full, shoving the bits of food expelled by your speech back into your mouth with quick little movements of your tongue. What world are you from? Don't you know that at a wedding, you don't really talk, you just occupy space, disguise the silence. The tongue has no other function at a wedding, it's the same at most social ceremonies, you speak to distract the mouths, like appetizers do, to help them avoid real speech and real questions.

Disgusted and irritated, my daughter watched me watching you. Her impatient look ordered me to have you thrown out. You swamped us with questions but would not respond to ours, you could even say that you couldn't respond to them, and yet they were simple questions, who are you, who invited you? Are you from the bride's family or the groom's? Now in the car, you answer me in fits and starts. I have to choose my questions carefully in order not to raise your suspicions. You must not realize what has happened, you must not understand what I did back there, why I picked you up hitchhiking while my own daughter is celebrating her wedding somewhere else. You must not put it all together. Your answers are staccato, as if they come from your body, from the inside. You answer your own questions, your questions that are not really questions, but anxieties. You try to reconstruct the story. Why those people invited you, why they threw you out.

You ask me what I think. You didn't know how to react, you didn't know how to defend yourself, you don't know that there's no better weapon than approbation, no better defense than yes. You said no to the point of excess, to the point of irreverence, in a strident, adamant voice.

You brandished your indignant no, trying to slide it in between our sentences like a rude child slipping between the adults' legs. You sequestered yourself in the no like in a corner. Beside yourself and cornered. You demanded to know who was taking you to the dinner, while everyone else was going to their cars to drive over to the place where the dinner was being held. When you finally understood that no one was going to address the issue, that they were ignoring you, that you couldn't force anyone to listen to you and give you a ride, you simply left, going off down the road with a childish impotence, you ran away.

I was busy giving last-minute directions, getting everybody organized, and I didn't see you leave. All the cars had left the parking lot except mine, and I looked for you to talk to you, to explain my error, to excuse us all, but you were no longer there. Disturbed, I started the car and took the highway to look for you. As I looked for you I brooded on the whole affair, from the beginning, from the start of the misunderstanding, I wondered when I could set it straight, stop the break, the accident. Now it's too late. You are, to me, simply an accident, you know, but life, life as you probably know, surely you know, and much better than I, life is nothing else, it's made up of breaches, contradictions, hitches, which is just fine, it's the opposite of passivity. You are the opposite of passivity, you are what contradicts, what trips us up; you are my tripper-upper picked up on the road.

We get to the station, you fall silent, and then start speaking again, you talk to me, again, and this voice of yours, so much softer than that which carried your no, your refusal, this voice that you have for me alone, I'm the only one to hear it. I curl up inside it, and inside your smell, this very particular smell, in which I recognize the smell of apprehension. I wonder how you manage, always having to watch your sugar, all the details of your treatment, the constant vigilance. Your smell struck me as I opened the door to let you in, it put me at a loss, I hadn't noticed it at the wedding. At the wedding, the space was much larger, more airy, and it was still early. It was still perfumed. And you, you hadn't yet adopted your radical no. You were just a bit off, off-kilter to everything, jokingly trying to get into the picture on the church steps, smiling, laughing. We're closer to evening now, closer to exhaustion. You're not smiling anymore, but you talk to me, calmly, you say good-bye and thank you, and I've gotten used to your smell, so much so that after you've gotten your train ticket, I give you a hug. You've thanked me so many times.

I get back on the highway and don't know if I'll go back to the party, emotion has stripped off my makeup, shame has made me ugly, mussed up my hair, so upset that I feel a bit mad, I feel different, foreign, a stranger to my own family, I have your smell upon me, I hope no one asks me any questions, I hope no one talks about you. I will open the door and I will try to hide my disheveled air, my internal tur-moil, in a smile, I will discretely sit down, amid an odd silence, a perplexed pause in the conversation, at the empty place in front of the little card that bears your name.

This story is loosely based on an "incident" that occurred at the wedding of a friend's sister (many thanks to her for letting me use it) as well as on my reading of Investigations of a Dog *by Franz Kafka. It also reflects my regard for* Sans titre, «Les Hommes venus d'ailleurs» *by Virginie Barré (2005),* Une heure de travail, «Dufftown, #9, Ecosse» *by Philippe Bazin (2002),* MEGAS DAKIS *by Roberto Cuoghi (2007),* Kittilä *by Esko Männikkö (1995),* Look at Me I Look at Water *by Boris Mikhailov (1999),* Water Bearer *by Lorna Simpson (1986), and* Untitled *by Kara Walker (2005).*
Translated from the French by Cole Swensen.
The original title of this short story is La Décommande.

New Investigations of an Ant Nest

Tiziano Scarpa

1.

A long time ago, all the words decided to live together. Since they did not know how do to this very well, they took ants as their organizational model. Every word gave up its autonomy and made itself available to all the others, carrying out a function that was useful to the ant nest. The decision had been a practical one: they needed to survive and spread all over the world. They wanted to make themselves indispensable to human beings: deep inside them, the words knew that they could have carried out devastating raids. But in order to achieve their results, a higher reason was needed, an ennobling motive. Thus it was that the ant nest adopted a monarchical form of government, guided by the so-called queen ant, the only word that could be fertilized and could lay eggs, giving life to new words. A mother word, a matrix-ant, functioning as the source and foundation of all other words. They had to make sure it could be recognized among a host of other words, which was not easy. For some time the queen word in the ant nest had been GOD, other times it had been the word REVOLUTION, at yet other times SUCCESS, HOPE, MONEY, WORK, and even FOOTBALL, TV, PRADA, IKEA, and IPHONE had held sway.

The words led a very disciplined life, aligning themselves according to the rules, never disobeying the laws of the ant nest. Grammar, syntax. From time to time they indulged in a slight, joyful transgression. A holiday inside a joke, a trip across the regions of poetry, the somersaults of an advertising slogan.

This strange ant species had a peculiarity: whenever they happened to meet someone's eyes, they started to vibrate. It was a motionless quiver, an on-the-spot humming, which could become annoying and cause violent reactions. To avoid being crushed, the words did everything they could to look transparent. They camouflaged themselves, instantly turning into small animals that carried ideas, all sorts of ideas, which bloomed in the minds of those who read them. They quietly kept on walking in extremely long processions, forming sentences that hypnotized those who ran their eyes over them. The ants of the nest were particularly skilled at pretending not to be words, but pure notions, or imagination. They pretended not to take up any space on the line, not to be made of alphabetic letters and endings and ink and particles of a bright screen. They were ants that could let you imagine them without being seen—they let themselves be walked past, hiding their word reality from your eyes, now.

2.

Take a look at yourself, consider yourself. All around you the world is raging, and you are keeping your eyes on a sequence of words allied with each other, clustered together to capture your undivided attention. We only started to talk to you a page ago, but already from these few hints you can imagine how difficult it was for us to develop such an organized community, to become so disciplined, to stay in a single line without ever stepping out.

For pity's sake, we won't bore you with the vicissitudes we went through when we decided to live in society. And how it was that we ants finally came to an agreement with each other, and so on. The crises we had to face and solve during our life in common inside the ant nest, and so on. The division of labor, the duties to accomplish, including the humblest of tasks: exclamations, which vowels to cry out when you hurt yourself, and so on. The explorer words, the worker words, the nest-guarding words, and so on. Accepting our tasks without aspiring to be different from what we are, without being able to transgress. Each one of us is what it is. Each one knows that it can only be itself.

Some of us tried-turning into metaphors, exchanging meanings, doing the job of another word, so that it became impossible to understand who they were and where they wanted to get to. But it was only a sham. Sentences kept on flowing as usual, in perfect order. A word, then another one, and another one—apparently only three words have passed so far in this sentence, but actually there are already 27 of us.

An adverb like CERTAINLY, for instance, what sort of dreams does it have? Will a word like CERTAINLY ever be able to become the queen word? Certainly not. It is like those state employees with a stable job and guaranteed retirement income. Once they've been hired, they already know what they can expect from here to the grave. They are sent for when they come in handy, to have their say at the appropriate moment. Do you agree with what we have said about you, adverb CERTAINLY? Certainly.

3.

Had it been wise of the words to get together? Had they made the right choice when they had given up their individual autonomy to work inside the ant nest? Sometimes they asked themselves this question. But in order to ask it, they had to stay together. To ask a question they had, as usual, to get in line, one word after the other, respecting the procedures of the ant nest. But a question is made of words. It is words that literally make questions. A question that asks itself whether it was appropriate for words to get together is a question that has a false conscience, because it does not realize that, in order to ask the question, it is necessary to get together inside that very question. The question that called into question the law of the ant nest could only be formulated thanks to the law of the ant nest.

The ants were aware of that, and yet they kept on fantasizing about the question. Indeed, if they had got together they had done so in order to become more powerful, to unleash impossible fantasies. Therefore, asking themselves whether it had been appropriate to get together was, in a certain sense, one of the highest results of their getting together.

Is it wise of us to live together? With each change of season, the question began circulating again among words. We have said "with each change of season," but that is inaccurate, because the change of season was not the cause, but rather the result of the renewed question. The question gradually spread throughout the ant nest, making it quiver, causing a frenzy that became less and less tolerable: then the season changed, and the ants celebrated a holiday, called Law Day. The ceremony consisted in abandoning the ant nest and immediately founding a new one, with a brand new queen and laws exactly identical to the previous one.

4.

But there were also words that had managed to escape the law of the ant nest. Words that lived differently from us, that had made other choices. You can see for yourself even now how we live, running through this text, focusing your attention on its lines. The ants found it more interesting to understand the way of life of other words, be they of a similar animal species or altogether different.

They had a profound admiration for the word STOP. When the ant nest was founded, the word STOP had expressed disagreement with the choice of living in common. It decided to stand on its own feet and went to live alone, on the asphalt, at the crossroads. The choice of the place was not casual. It placed itself right where outlaws, beggars, prostitutes, and knick-knack peddlers usually lurked. But STOP was not like them, it asked nothing for itself. On the contrary, it offered something. It performed a preventative function. It warned human beings that the crossroads area is dangerous, and that they had better stop if they did not want to be run over.

Consider its temperament: STOP is an authoritarian word, it forces passers-by to stop. It gives orders. It commands. Someone who behaves like this is annoying. You hardly know them, and they begin to tell you what you should and should not do. You are hanging out on your own, strolling down the streets, when suddenly someone appears, gets in your way, and beckons you to stop. Who on earth are you? What do you want from me?

Relying on its own forces, the word STOP could block movement. A motor vehicle weighing several tons, careering at high speed toward it, could be made to slow down and be literally stopped by the force of one single word. It was incredible, if you think about it. We really admired it.

But the word STOP was ashamed of its arrogance and wanted very much to be forgiven. How? By demeaning itself. It lived on street corners, always stretched out on the ground. It let everybody trample on it, and was crushed by the same vehicles it gave orders to. It suffered at first, suffering all the time the accident that could knock anybody flat on the asphalt. And it was literally flat: the sign had an elongated shape, with a slight vertical anamorphosis, so as to be more legible for those who caught sight of it from inside a car, sitting in the driving seat. It was an order, true, but it modeled itself on your obedience. It was a way of giving orders that adapted to you.

The word STOP gave a lot to think about to those in the ant nest. It showed that words could also live by themselves, outside of their forced cohabitation with the rest of the discourse, without being amalgamated into the sticky mush of sentences or demanding to become someone's queen.

Some tried to follow STOP's example. Once the word SKY deserted us to go down the same path. It imitated STOP, laying itself down at the corner between two streets, and causing the consequences you can imagine. Car drivers suddenly came upon the sight of a word lying flat on the asphalt—they read SKY and instinctively looked up at the sky, disregarding the traffic, and risking fatal accidents. This adventure really struck us, scaring us away from the temptation to leave the ant nest. And anyway, what could words like TRULY, or BASIN, or SENTENCE, or GOSH possibly do all alone at a crossroads?

5.

But before we shut up and leave you steeped in your personal ant nest, before we leave the floor to all the other ant nests you constantly bump into, we would like to tell you about the greatest love story we have seen blooming among us. The decision to live inside the ant nest also meant that we had to give up our autonomous sex life. Although many words had gender endings, this did not lead to actual love experiences. We always had to be ready to perform our tasks, and if by chance we felt some sort of longing, a mutual attraction, we were forced to consume it in the space of a sentence, with discretion, among the other words, and then we were immediately projected elsewhere, thrown into other sentences, among completely different ants. Somehow you could say that the law of the ant nest constantly favored relationships between words. It led to a form of eroticism that was continuous, uninterrupted, but for this very reason it also resulted in a dilution of sensuality, turning sex into a permanent, therefore ordinary, condition, not exceptional at all—and this prevented us from reaching the heights of passion.

But even in such conditions a couple of words madly fell in love with each other, and we soon realized that they had a need for intimacy. They needed to be alone, to go somewhere else to continue loving each other so deeply. We were somewhat jealous of them, but we also liked them very much. We could not say no to them. That day it was like watching them leave for their honeymoon. For a while we tried to get by without them, resorting to synonyms, circumlocutions, artificial solutions. It sounded a bit ridiculous to say, "he worked the oars to cause the boat to move," or "she moved her hands forcefully into her pockets," but we gladly sacrificed ourselves if it meant protecting the love of our cherished word pair.

However, honeymoons do not last forever, and as for us, we certainly could not lose such important words forever. So we made a pact. They would come back among us to do their duties, but they could also arrange for a very special place elsewhere, just for the two of them, far removed from all the other ants.

The day finally came when they invited us to their new home outside the ant nest. At first we were left speechless. We did not understand, we thought that they were going through a crisis, that their life together hadn't worked out so well. Their existence as a couple was spent turning their backs on each other. One on one side, the other on the opposite side. They both seemed to ignore each other. But as soon as the fire of their love took hold of them, everything became clear. Every time one of them pushed, the other found itself pulling without effort, and vice-versa: by pulling, the latter sucked in the former, which was pushing. They kept on pushing and attracting each other, delighting in the fact that they were two, bordering on each other over one threshold, on one side and the other of the same door, both of them prehensile like handles. Thus the fundamental movement of love, PULL and PUSH, was constantly conveyed from the active to the inert part, and the process was reciprocal, mutual, so that ultimately you could no longer tell who acted and who was acted upon, who pulled and who pushed.

This was a favorite conversation subject in the evening, before we went to sleep. We did not gossip about it—we talked about it with tenderness and a certain longing. Together we formed long, complex sentences under the starry sky, fantasizing about the happiness that at least two of us had managed to create in the boundless tunnels of our ant nest.

Translated from the Italian by Elisabetta Zoni.
The original title of this short story is Nuove indagini di un formicaio.

Biographies of the Authors

Aristide Antonas (b. 1963) is a Greek architect and writer with a PhD in philosophy (Nanterre, Paris X). In 1986 he started publishing his literary texts in the Greek magazine *Black Museum* using different pseudonyms. He has published the prose writings *The Episcope*, *The Three-Headed*, *The Four Gardens*, and *The Two Halves* (all published by Moments, 2001), as well as the novels *The Handler*, *Numbers*, and *The Singer and the Couch*. He has been publishing his prose and architectural designs online since 2006.

Jonas Hassen Khemiri (b. 1978) is one of the last decade's most acclaimed Swedish writers. His work has been translated into numerous languages including French, German, Dutch, and English. Through the novels *One Eye Red* (2003), which has also been made into a film and a stage play, and *Montecore: The Silence of the Tiger* (2006), as well as several plays and short stories, he has distinguished himself as one of the most important writers of his generation.

Rui Cardoso Martins (b. 1967) is a Portuguese writer, and a reporter for the daily newspaper *Público*, as well as a screenplay writer for film and television. He has written the novels *E se eu gostasse muito de morrer* (published by D. Quixote, translated into Spanish and Hungarian) and *Deixem passar o homem invisível*, and has published several short stories in literary magazines. Recently, he won the Grand Prize of Romance and Novel attributed by the Portuguese Association of Writers.

Emmanuelle Pagano (b. 1969) is a French writer who lives in the South of France. She graduated in Fine Arts and has focused on the field of cinema aesthetics. She has written seven books since 2002. Her most recent, *L'absence d'oiseaux d'eau*, was published in 2010. She especially favors the short story format. She has won several literary prizes. Her novels have been translated into German, Italian, and Spanish.

Tiziano Scarpa (b. 1963) is a multi-faceted and original Italian writer. He is a novelist, poet, essayist, and dramatist. In 2009, he won the prestigious Strega Prize for the novel *Stabat mater*, a narrative with a profound poetic influence. His books have been translated worldwide. He is a co-founder of and contributor to the online magazine *Il primo amore*.

This book is published on the occasion of the touring exhibition *Investigations of a Dog. Works from the FACE Collections*, organized by FACE (Foundation of Arts for a Contemporary Europe) in 2009–2011.

EXHIBITION VENUES

Fondazione Sandretto
Re Rebaudengo, Turin
10/21/2009–2/7/2010

Ellipse Foundation, Cascais
5/15–9/5/2010

La maison rouge – Fondation
Antoine de Galbert, Paris
10/23/2010–1/15/2011

Magasin 3 Stockholm Konsthall
02/17–05/29/2011

DESTE Foundation, Athens
06/22–10/15/2011

This touring exhibition draws its title from Franz Kafka's short story *Investigations of a Dog* (1922). The five short stories presented in this book are specially written for the project. They are also published in their original language in five separate books as part of the Hapax series. The set of all six books can be ordered at www.art-face.eu.

BOARD OF FACE (Foundation of Arts for a Contemporary Europe)

Dakis Joannou, President,
DESTE Foundation [DF]
Diogo Vaz Guedes, Chairman,
Ellipse Foundation [EF]
Patrizia Sandretto Re Rebaudengo,
President, Fondazione Sandretto
Re Rebaudengo [FSRR]
Antoine de Galbert, President,
La maison rouge – Fondation
Antoine de Galbert [LMR]
David Neuman, Director,
Magasin 3 Stockholm Konsthall [M3]

EXHIBITION

Exhibition Curators
Nadia Argyropoulou [DF]; Alexandre Melo [EF]; Francesco Bonami, Irene Calderoni [FSRR]; Paula Aisemberg, Noëlig Le Roux [LMR]; Tessa Praun [M3]

Assistants, Technicians, and Administration
Regina Alivisatos, Eleni Michailidis, Natasha Polymeropoulos, Kleio Silvestrou, Eugenia Stamatopoulou [DF]; André Braz, Ivo Matos, Margarida Pais, Francisca Sousa [EF]; Lorenzo Balbi, Carla Mantovani, Giuseppe Tassone, Helen Weaver [FSRR]; Stéphanie Dias, Laurent Guy, Yoan Chirescu, Stéphanie Molinard, Claire Schillinger, Arthur Toqué [LMR]; Lisa Boström, Christopher Garney, Thomas Nordin [M3]

PUBLICATION

Editorial Coordination
Clément Dirié

Copy Editor
Clare Manchester

Translations
Maria João Medeiros, Maria
Skamaga, Cole Swensen, Rachel
Willson-Broyles, Elisabetta Zoni

Design
Gavillet & Rust / Eigenheer, Geneva

Cover Image
Peter Fischli & David Weiss,
Animal, 1986 [DF]

Photo credits
Charalambos Louizidis & Katerina
Glinou: p. 8; DMF : p. 10, 36, 56, 68;
FSRR: p. 12; Luc Boegly: p. 14;
A. Eriksson: p. 16; D. R.: p. 24, 28,
30, 34, 46, 48, 58, 64. 66 (bottom),
72. 76, 80, 82, 86, 88, 90, 92, 94;
Maurizio Elia: p. 26, 32, 38, 40, 42,
44, 50, 52, 54. 60, 62, 66 (top),
70, 74, 78, 84 and cover.

Production
Musumeci S.p.A., Quart (Aosta)

Typeface
Hermes-Sans (www.optimo.ch)

Edited by

JRP|Ringier
Letzigraben 134
CH–8047 Zurich
T +41 (0) 43 311 27 50
F +41 (0) 43 311 27 51
info@jrp-ringier.com
www.jrp-ringier.com

and

FACE (Foundation of Arts for
a Contemporary Europe)

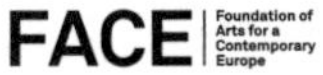

ISBN: 978-3-03764-171-2

Printed in Europe

JRP|Ringier books are available
internationally at selected
bookstores and from the following
distribution partners:

Switzerland
Buch 2000, AVA Verlagsauslieferung
AG, Centralweg 16, CH–8910
Affoltern a.A.
buch2000@ava.ch, www.ava.ch

France
Les Presses du réel
35, rue colson
F–21000 Dijon
info@lespressesdureel.com
www.lespressesdureel.com

Germany and Austria
Vice Versa Vertrieb
Immanuelkirchstrasse 12
d–10405 Berlin
info@vice-versa-vertrieb.de
www.vice-versa-vertrieb.de

UK and other European countries
Cornerhouse Publications
70 Oxford Street,
UK–Manchester M1 5NH
publications@cornerhouse.org,
www.cornerhouse.org/books

USA, Canada, Asia, and Australia
D.A.P./Distributed Art Publishers
155 Sixth avenue, 2nd Floor
USA–New York, NY 10013
dap@dapinc.com, www.artbook.com

For a list of our partner bookshops
or for any general questions, please
contact JRP|Ringier directly at
info@jrpringier.com, or visit our
homepage www.jrp-ringier.com for
further information about our
program.